GREEN LANTERN
SECRET ORIGIN

IVAN REIS
+
DAVE-CO

SECRET ORIGIN

Geoff Johns
Writer

Ivan Reis
Penciller

Oclair Albert
Inker

Randy Mayor
Colors

Rob Leigh
Letters

With
Julio Ferreira Partial Inker Book 3
Ivan Reis Partial Inker Book 6

Original Se **e McCaig**

Cover art by Ivan Reis and Dave McCaig

GREEN LANTERN: SECRET ORIGIN

DC Comics, 1700 Broadway, New York, NY 10019
A Warner Bros. Entertainment Company
Printed in USA. First Printing.

ISBN: 978-1-4012-1990-1
SC ISBN: 978-1-4012-2017-4

IVAN REIS
+
DAVE-CO

SECRET ORIGIN

BOOK ONE

"WHAT ARE YOU AFRAID OF?"
PEOPLE LIKE TO ASK ME THAT. WHEN THEY DO, THEY HAVE THIS KNOWING GRIN ON THEIR FACES. AS IF THEY EXPECT ME TO ANSWER, "NOTHING."
I HUMOR THEM MOST OF THE TIME, BECAUSE THAT'S WHAT THEY WANT ME TO SAY.
"I'M NOT AFRAID OF ANYTHING."
JORDAN

THEY THINK I WAS BORN WITHOUT FEAR.
THEY'RE WRONG.
THEY THINK THIS RING GIVES ME THE POWER TO DO ANYTHING.
THEY'RE WRONG ABOUT THAT TOO.

BEFORE I WAS GIVEN THE GREATEST WEAPON IN THE UNIVERSE, BEFORE I JOURNEYED TO THE STARS--
--MY DAD GAVE ME THE POWER TO DO ANYTHING.
HE TOLD ME I COULD BE WHATEVER I WANTED TO BE.

AND I WANTED TO
BE JUST LIKE HIM.
GO, DAD!

JIM WASN'T OLD ENOUGH TO GO WATCH HIM FLY. JACK WAS TOO OLD TO CARE.
I DIDN'T WANT TO BE ANYWHERE ELSE.
EVERY DAY, I WENT TO FERRIS AIR.
SOMETIMES I'D GET TO SCHOOL LATE. SOMETIMES I'D LEAVE SCHOOL EARLY. SOMETIMES I'D NEVER GO TO SCHOOL AT ALL.
THOSE DAYS, I'D WATCH DAD FLY ALL MORNING. THEN WE'D SIT IN HIS COCKPIT AND SHARE MY BROWN BAG LUNCH.
MOM USED TO WONDER WHY I ASKED FOR ROAST BEEF AND HORSERADISH. I NEVER ATE HORSERADISH AT HOME.
BUT DAD LOVED IT.
THAT JACKET LOOKS TOO BIG.
HE ASKED ME TO HOLD IT.
WHO DID?
MY DAD'S FLYING THAT PLANE.
Hmph.
MY DAD OWNS THAT PLANE.
WE OWN ALL OF THEM.

I'M HAL JORDAN.
I'M CAROL FERRIS.
I'M GOING TO BE A PILOT WHEN I GROW UP.
REALLY? ME TOO!
JORDAN

WELL, I'M GOING TO OWN MY OWN PLANE.

DANGER
DO NOT ENTER
THAT'D BE COOL.
HEY! YOU'RE NOT SUPPOSED TO GO IN THERE. THE SIGN SAYS SO.
YOU WANNA COME?
NO. YOU'RE GOING TO GET IN TROUBLE.

I'M NOT AFRAID OF GETTING IN TROUBLE, CAROL.

DAMMIT. I'M HAVING SOME PROBLEMS HERE, FERRIS. OIL'S GETTIN' EATEN UP QUICK. I THINK THE LAST OF MY TORQUE PINS JUST FAILED.
I THOUGHT THIS WAS SENT TO I-LEVEL REPAIR.
IT WAS.
DADDY!
DADDY, THAT BOY IS BREAKING THE RULES!
ONE MINUTE, HONEY, OKAY?
I NEED TO BRING IT IN. AWAY FROM THE CROWD.

THERE'S NO EXTERNAL LEAKAGE. THE INVESTORS ARE WATCHING.
THAT'S FIFTEEN-MILLION DOLLARS AND OUR LAST SIX YEARS OF DEVELOPMENT YOU HAVE IN THE AIR.
KEEP IT FLYING, JORDAN.
THIS THING'S GOING DOWN, FERRIS.
ON TOP OF YOU, COAST CITY, OR RIGHT HERE...
...AND RIGHT HERE NO ONE ELSE GETS HURT.

WHEN YOUR WORST FEAR HAPPENS IN FRONT OF YOUR EYES--
JORDAN
DAD.

--I THOUGHT THERE WAS NOTHING LEFT TO BE AFRAID OF.
MOM THOUGHT THERE WAS EVERYTHING.

YAAHOOO!
KEN ARDEN FLEW IN THE AIR FORCE WITH DAD AND CARL FERRIS. AFTER DAD DIED, ARDEN STARTED HIS OWN AEROSPACE TESTING FACILITY.
THAT WAS PERFECT FOR ME. I SWORE TO MOM THAT I'D NEVER GO TO FERRIS AIR AGAIN--
--BUT I CAUGHT THE BUS TO ARDEN AVIATION EVERY CHANCE I GOT. THERE WAS A BROKEN LOCK ON THE SOUTH GATE THAT THEY DIDN'T USE ANYMORE. IT WAS EASY ENOUGH TO GET IN.
EASY ENOUGH TO CLIMB THE LADDER UP TO THE TOP OF HANGAR 3, TOO.
THERE WASN'T A BETTER VIEW IN THE WORLD.
YEAH!
HAL?!
FWOOOOSH
HAL, HOW IN THE WORLD DID YOU--?
I JUMPED.
DON'T WORRY, MR. ARDEN, I CAN GET DOWN MYSELF. IT'S LIKE A GIANT FIREMAN'S POLE!
DON'T YOU MOVE!

I'M SO SORRY, KEN.
IT'S OKAY, JESSICA...

...HE'S JUST GOT A LOT OF HIS FATHER IN HIM.

HOW MANY TIMES HAVE YOU PROMISED ME YOU WOULDN'T GO TO THE AIRFIELDS, HAL?
YOU SAID FERRIS AIR.

YOU ARE NOT ALLOWED ANYWHERE NEAR A PLANE, DO YOU UNDERSTAND ME, YOUNG MAN?
DO YOU?

YES, MA'AM.
I DIDN'T UNDERSTAND HER.
AND SHE DIDN'T UNDERSTAND ME.

NO ONE DID.
NICE GOING, JERK.
SHUT UP, JACK.
MOM WAS FREAKING OUT WHEN MR. ARDEN CALLED. SHE ALMOST HAD A HEART ATTACK!

OW.
YOU SCARE MOM LIKE THAT AGAIN AND THERE'S PLENTY MORE.

DON'T FIGHT! DON'T FIGHT!
WE'RE NOT, JIM.
WE AREN'T MOVING.
BUCKLE UP.
BETTER SAFE THAN SORRY. MOM SAYS SO.

BUCKLE UP.
BEFORE MOM HAS TO TELL YOU TO.

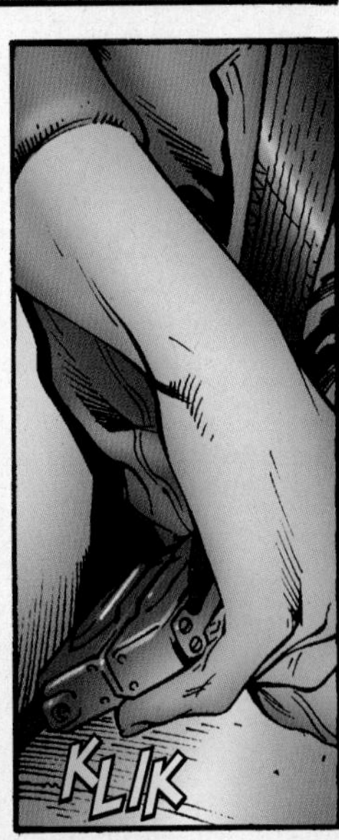
KLIK

I NEVER MEANT TO HURT ANYONE. NOT THE DOZENS OF TIMES MOM FOUND ME AT ARDEN.
AND NOT THAT NIGHT.
11:59
MIDNIGHT! ALL RIGHT!
To My Brother HAL
HAL?! HAPPY BIRTH--

SON?

CAN I HELP YOU?

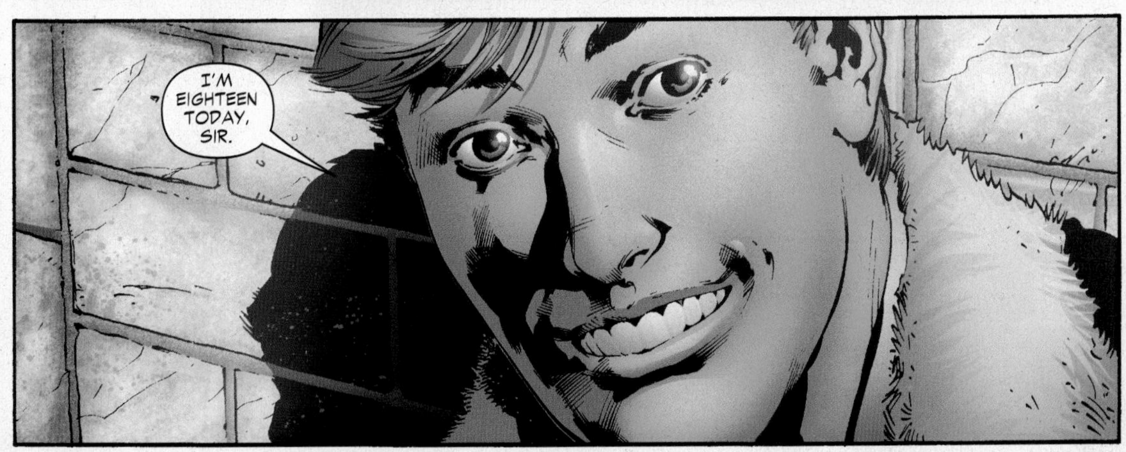
I'M EIGHTEEN TODAY, SIR.

ARMED FORCES CAREER CENTER
US ARMY
US MARINE CORPS
2814
AIR FORCE RECRUITING SERVICE
AIR FORCE
WELL, THEN--
--HAPPY BIRTHDAY.

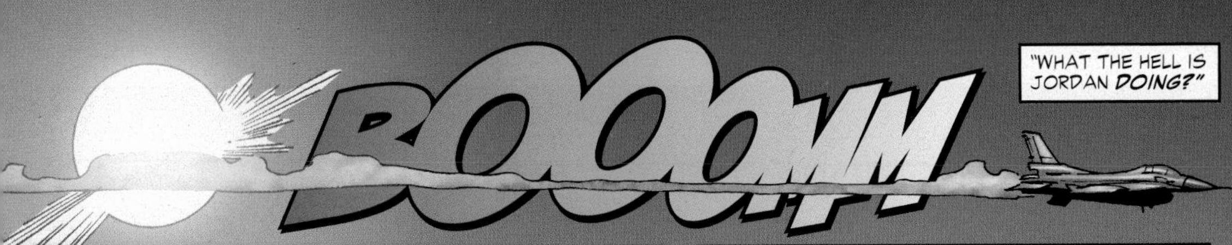
"WHAT THE HELL IS JORDAN DOING?"
BOOOMM!

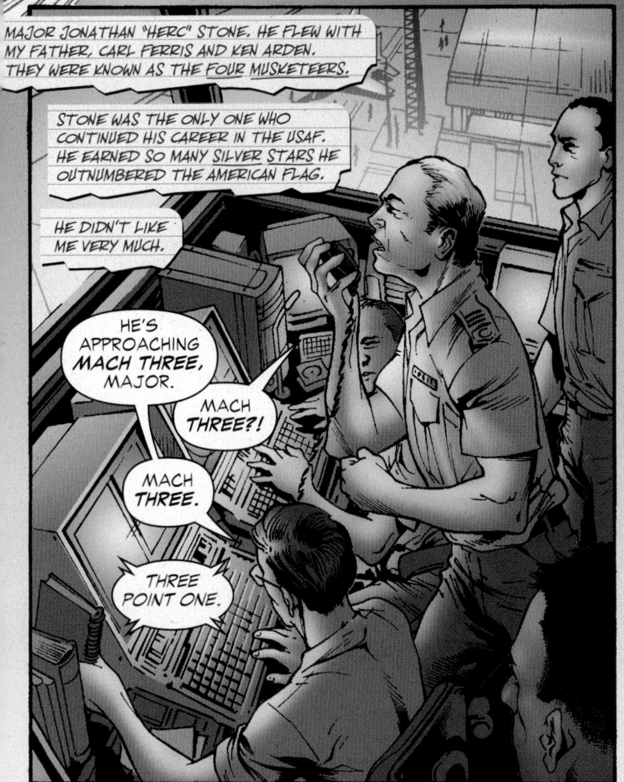
MAJOR JONATHAN "HERC" STONE. HE FLEW WITH MY FATHER, CARL FERRIS AND KEN ARDEN. THEY WERE KNOWN AS THE FOUR MUSKETEERS.
STONE WAS THE ONLY ONE WHO CONTINUED HIS CAREER IN THE USAF. HE EARNED SO MANY SILVER STARS HE OUTNUMBERED THE AMERICAN FLAG.
HE DIDN'T LIKE ME VERY MUCH.
HE'S APPROACHING MACH THREE, MAJOR.
MACH THREE?!
MACH THREE.
THREE POINT ONE.

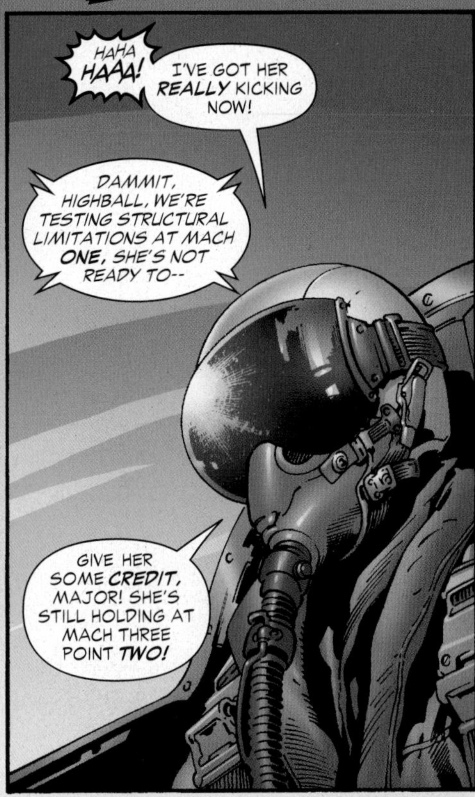
HAHA HAAA!
I'VE GOT HER REALLY KICKING NOW!
DAMMIT, HIGHBALL, WE'RE TESTING STRUCTURAL LIMITATIONS AT MACH ONE, SHE'S NOT READY TO--
GIVE HER SOME CREDIT, MAJOR! SHE'S STILL HOLDING AT MACH THREE POINT TWO!

MACH THREE POINT THR--!
RRRRRMMMMMBBBBLLLL
TINGG TINGG TINGG
HEY, STONE...

...SHE CAN HANDLE A *HAIR* PAST MACH THREE POINT TWO.

COAST CITY WAS LESS THAN HALF AN HOUR FROM EDWARDS. TWENTY MINUTES FROM FORT ROCK.
AND THERE WAS ALWAYS A BATTLESHIP OR THREE IN THE HARBOR.
COAST CITY WAS A MILITARY TOWN.
AND FRIDAY NIGHT, IT ALWAYS LIT UP LIKE A ROCKET. THAT NIGHT, IT WAS PACKED BY THE AIR FORCE AND THE MARINES, READY FOR TAKE OFF.
...YOU'RE THE BEST SHOT IN THE CORPS. WE'D HATE TO LOSE YOU.
...YOU'RE SCREWED, HIGHBALL. YOU PISSED OFF STONE. YOU INVALIDATED HIS ENTIRE TWO-YEAR PROGRAM.
I SAVED THE AIR FORCE TWO YEARS OF TEST FLIGHTS. THE F-16'S READY FOR COMBAT NOW, ROCKET-MAN.
YOU DESTROYED A THIRTY MILLION DOLLAR JET TO PROVE THAT?
IF THAT'S WHAT IT TAKES TO GET OUR PILOTS IN THE SAFEST EQUIPMENT SOONER THAN LATER, FINE.
STONE'S GONNA TAKE THIS OUT ON ALL OF US.

THAT'S WHY THE DRINKS ARE ON ME.
LET GO.
YOU'RE COMING HOME WITH ME, CINDY.
NO, I'M NOT.
I'M NOT GOING ANYWHERE!
YOU'RE COMING NOW OR I'LL SNAP YOUR NECK.
HEY, WARTHOG. THE LADY DOESN'T WANT TO GO WITH YOU.
MIND YOUR OWN BUSINESS, FLYBOY.
THAT HURTS--
--OWW!

KRRAKK

YOU SEE THAT, STEWART?
THAT JET JOCKEY JUST KNOCKED DOWN ONE OF OURS.
HERE WE GO.

HERE WE GO.
HEN IT COMES TO WAR, WE MIGHT ALL BE ON HE SAME SIDE. BUT IF YOU THINK THERE'S NO TERSERVICE RIVALRY BETWEEN THE MERICAN ARMED FORCES--
--YOU'RE AS SHARP AS A JARHEAD.
YOU SHOULD BE HAPPY.
THIS IS MORE FIGHTING THAN THE AIR FORCE WILL SHOW YOU ALL YEAR.
THEN I BETTER MAKE IT COUNT.

HAL?

JIM?
IT'S PAST *TWO* IN THE MORNING. WHAT ARE YOU DOING--?
I KNOW THIS IS YOUR HANGOUT. I'VE BEEN WAITING FOR YOU. LIKE ALWAYS.
BRO, I--

MOM'S DYING.

WHAT IS IT?
CANCER. IT STARTED IN THE PANCREAS. AND IT'S *BAD.*
I NEED TO SEE HER.
YOU *CAN'T.*
WHAT DO YOU MEAN I CAN'T?

YOU KNOW WHAT MOM SAID. AS LONG AS YOU'RE IN THE AIR FORCE--
THIS IS *DIFFERENT,* JIM.

THE DOCTORS SAID THE STATE SHE'S IN, ANYTHING *UPSETTING* COULD TRIGGER ALL SORTS OF *PHYSICAL* PROBLEMS.
JACK WON'T LET YOU.
I CAN'T LET YOU EITHER.

THE NEXT MORNING, I GOT TO BASE EARLY. INSTEAD OF REPORTING RIGHT TO STONE'S OFFICE, I TOOK AN UNAUTHORIZED JOYRIDE.
...THE LAST TIME THE AIR FORCE LOST THIS MANY JETS IN ONE WEEK WE WERE AT WAR IN VIETNAM.
NOW I'VE GOT TO CALL THE PENTAGON AND EXPLAIN HOW WE LOST A THIRTY MILLION DOLLAR FIGHTER ON A DAMN TEST FLIGHT TO DETERMINE...
..."STRUCTURAL LIMITATIONS OF THE F-16 AT MACH ONE." THIS WASN'T EVEN A COMBAT SIMULATION!
IT WAS THE FIRST TIME I DIDN'T SMILE IN THE AIR.
WHEN I LANDED, STONE WAS WAITING FOR ME.
YOU MAY BE THE "BEST" PILOT ON PAPER, BUT IN REALITY YOU'RE THE MOST EXPENSIVE AND THE MOST DANGEROUS.
IT'S TIME YOU USE THAT LUMP ON YOUR SHOULDERS ONCE IN AWHILE.
STONE'S WORDS WERE JUST A FOG AROUND ME. LIKE JACK'S.
BUT I ALWAYS LISTENED TO JIM. AND THAT'S ALL I WAS HEARING.
"MOM'S DYING."
I JUST TOOK HER FOR A SPIN, MAJOR.
WITHOUT CLEARANCE AND WITHOUT AUTHORIZATION, JOYRIDING LIKE IT WAS YOUR LAST FLIGHT.
IT WAS. I KNEW IT WAS.
I COULDN'T SAY IT. I COULDN'T WALK AWAY. I COULDN'T QUIT.

I HAD TO FIND ANOTHER WAY OUT.
ANOTHER BAD CHOICE IN A LIFE FULL OF THEM.

HAL? HOW DID YOU...?
I CAME TO SEE MOM. YOU CAN TELL HER I WAS DISCHARGED, JIM. I'M *OUT* OF THE AIR FORCE.
YOU CAN TELL HER I KEPT MY PROMISE.
HAL, THERE WAS A COMPLICATION THIS AFTERNOON...

...MOM'S *GONE.*
WHAT? WHAT HAPPENED?

YOU KILLED HER.
JACK?
AFTER YOU *RAN AWAY*, SHE SPENT HER *LIFE* WORRYING.
SHE *HEARD* ABOUT ALL THE *CLOSE CALLS*. ALL THE *CRASHES*.

YOU KILLED MOM!
JACK! THIS IS TOUGH FOR *ALL* OF US--
SINCE WHEN IS *ANYTHING* TOUGH FOR HAL, JIM? WHEN DAD DIED *I* TOOK CARE OF MOM. I GOT A JOB TO HELP.

WHEN HAL RAN AWAY I LEFT COLLEGE. I MOVED HOME.
I GAVE MY *LIFE* FOR OUR FAMILY JUST LIKE MOM.

I WAS DAD'S SON. JIM WAS MOM'S. JACK WAS ALWAYS ON HIS OWN PATH...
WHEN HAS HAL *EVER* GIVEN THIS FAMILY *ANYTHING?*
...BUT I TOOK HIM OFF IT.

I WAS NEVER A GOOD BROTHER TO ANYONE.
NOK NOK
GLASS

JIM?
COME ON IN--
I CAN'T.
SUSAN'S WAITING IN THE CAR.
To My Brother HAL

WHAT'S *THIS?*
SOMETHING I WISH I COULD'VE GIVEN YOU A *LONG* TIME AGO.
I THOUGHT NO ONE UNDERSTOOD ME.
I WAS WRONG.
To My Brother HAL
I'D BEEN DISHONORABLY DISCHARGED. I TORE MY FAMILY APART.
I STARED AT THAT PICTURE OF ME AND DAD ALL NIGHT. WONDERING...

...WHERE THE HELL DO I GO FROM HERE?
THERE IS NO ESCAPE.

THAT IS WHY I HAVE RETURNED TO THIS FESTERING PIT OF A PLANET, QULL. I CAN HEAR THE SADISTIC LAUGHTER YOU DEMONS SHARE OVER THE HORROR THAT APPROACHES OTHERS.
YOU KNOW THAT, DON'T YOU, ABIN SUR? YOU BELIEVE OUR PROPHECIES.
I WILL STOP THAT HORROR. I WANT TO KNOW MORE ABOUT THE PROPHECIES YOU HAVE SEEN.

QUIET, QULL!
YOU HAVE TOLD ABIN SUR ENOUGH!
THOSE SECRETS REMAIN WITH US, GREEN LANTERN!

I HAVE HAD ENOUGH, ATRORCITUS!
YOU DO NOT GET TO CHOOSE WHEN YOU TALK TO ME AND WHEN YOU DO NOT.
CHUNK
AAARRG!

I WILL KNOW EVERYTHING YOU KNOW, DEMONS. ABOUT THE FATE OF THE UNIVERSE. ABOUT COSMIC REVELATIONS.
AND ABOUT "THE BLACKEST NIGHT."

BOOK TWO

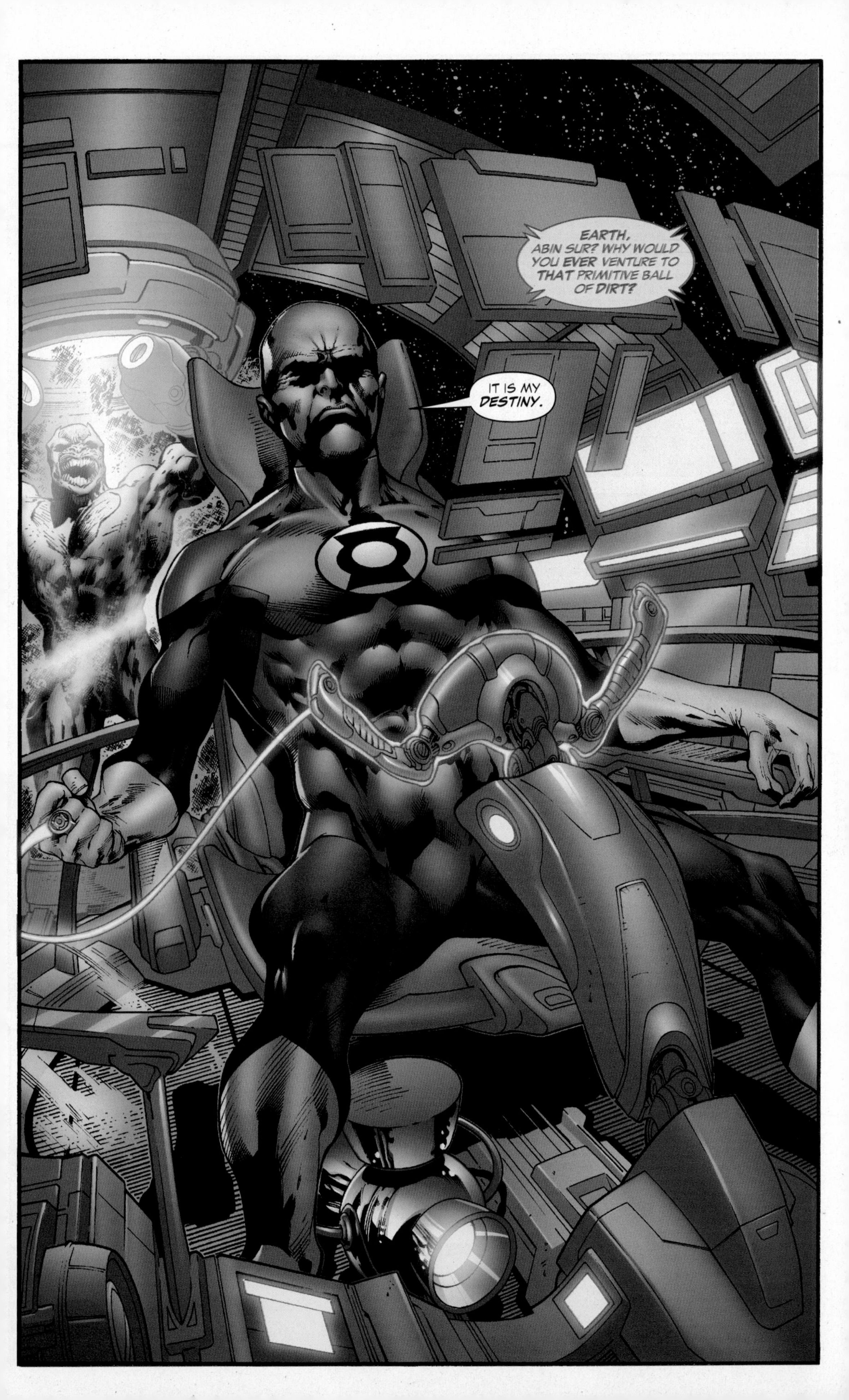
EARTH, ABIN SUR? WHY WOULD YOU EVER VENTURE TO THAT PRIMITIVE BALL OF DIRT?
IT IS MY DESTINY.

ACCORDING TO THE PROPHECY, EARTH IS THE BIRTHPLACE OF THE BLACK. THE ANTITHESIS OF THE EMOTIONAL SPECTRUM.
THE EMPTINESS THAT IS SAID TO ONE DAY CONSUME ALL LIGHT AND ALL LIFE.
"THE BLACKEST NIGHT" AGAIN, ABIN?
I AM INCREASINGLY WORRIED ABOUT YOU, MY FRIEND. YOU HAVE BECOME OBSESSED WITH THESE LIES.

AND NOW YOU FLY USING A SHIP RATHER THAN RELYING ON YOUR RING.

IT HAS BEEN FORETOLD MY RING WILL FAIL ME WHEN I MOST NEED IT.
"FORETOLD" BY THE PRISONERS OF THE PLANET YSMAULT. THOSE DEMONS WEAVE THEIR TALES IN AN ATTEMPT TO INSTILL FEAR INTO YOUR HEART AND THE GREEN LANTERN CORPS.
ALTHOUGH THE GUARDIANS FORBID FURTHER DISCUSSION, I WILL FIND PROOF OF THIS INEVITABLE RISE OF DARKNESS.

ATROCITUS WILL LEAD ME TO THE PLACE THAT WILL GIVE BIRTH TO THE BLACK.
I WILL ONLY LEAD YOU TO YOUR DEATH, GREEN LANTERN!
ATROCITUS IS IN YOUR CUSTODY? YOU FREED HIM FROM HIS CRUCIFIX ON YSMAULT? THE GUARDIANS WILL HAVE YOUR RING IF THEY DISCOVER THIS.

WISH ME LUCK THEN.
...ABIN...EVEN IF I AM WARY OF THE VALIDITY OF ANY OF THIS, YOU DO KNOW IF YOU FIND SOMETHING AND IF YOU NEED BACKUP...
...NOT EVEN THE GUARDIAN'S TERRITORIAL EDICT WILL KEEP ME OUT OF YOUR SECTOR.
THANK YOU, SINESTRO.
ABIN SUR-- GREEN LANTERN OF SPACE SECTOR 2814--
--OUT.

I WAS CAPTAIN HAL JORDAN.
NOW I WAS JUST HAL JORDAN.

WAS KICKED OUT OF THE AIR FORCE.
KICKED OUT OF MY FAMILY.
I HAD NOWHERE TO GO.
I WENT TO EVERY AIRFIELD IN COAST CITY, EXCEPT FOR FERRIS, LOOKING FOR WORK. KEN ARDEN WAS THE ONLY ONE WHO OFFERED ME A JOB.
BUT NOT IN THE COCKPIT.
ON THE GROUND.
ARDEN-AIR
HE TOOK ME ON AS A MECHANIC IN TRAINING. I KNEW EVERYTHING ABOUT HOW TO FLY. TOM KALMAKU TAUGHT ME EVERYTHING ABOUT WHY THE PLANE FLEW.
HEY, PIEFACE!
I CAN'T REMEMBER HOW I TREATED MY MECHANICS, BUT I SURE AS HELL HOPE IT WASN'T LIKE THIS.
"THE FLAMING SPEAR" NEEDS A NEW COAT OF WAX WHILE YOU'RE GASSIN' HER UP. AND HURRY THIS CRAP UP.
I NEED TO BE BACK IN THE AIR IN SIXTY, PIEFACE.
"PIEFACE"?
OH, I GET IT. AS IN "ESKIMO PIE." BECAUSE HE'S ASIAN.
YOU'RE PRETTY SMART FOR A POLACK, LAMINSKI.
AND YOU'RE PRETTY STUPID FOR A PILOT, JORDAN.
OR EX-PILOT.
JORDAN

DON'T LET LAMINSKI GET TO YOU, HAL.
...HAL?
WHAT'RE YOU STARIN' AT?

THAT PLANE.
YEAH. TRASH HEAP'S SEEN BETTER DAYS. NOT GOOD FOR ANYTHIN' BUT PARTS.
I REMEMBER IT.
ASPEN AIR
YOU REMEMBER IT?

MY DAD FLEW FOR A LOT OF AIRFIELDS IN COAST CITY. HE TOOK ME UP WITH HIM IN THAT PLANE ONCE.
LONG TIME AGO.
"DAD. I'M SCARED."

DON'T WORRY. YOU'RE FLYING WITH ***ME***, SON.
YOU'VE NEVER FLOWN WITH ***ME***.

I NEED TO GET BACK IN THE AIR.

MARTIN "BISHOP" JORDAN. KEN "HIGH LIFE" ARDEN. JONATHAN "HERC" STONE. CARL "ROOK" FERRIS.
THEY CALLED THEMSELVES THE FOUR MUSKETEERS WHEN THEY WERE IN THE AIR FORCE. EVENTUALLY, ALL OF THEM EXCEPT STONE LEFT TO WORK IN THE PRIVATE SECTOR.
I'D BEEN SNEAKING ONTO ARDEN'S AIRFIELD SINCE I WAS A KID.
THAT'S WHY HE CUT ME A BREAK WITH A JOB. HE KNEW DAD. HE KNEW MOM.
HE KNEW ME.
NO.

BUT I'M TEN TIMES THE PILOT LAMINSKI IS.
YOU'RE ALSO TEN TIMES AS DANGEROUS. THE PLANES YOU BROUGHT DOWN IN THE AIR FORCE DIDN'T VANISH OFF YOUR RECORD.
MAYBE I PUSHED IT A LITTLE. I WON'T--
PUTTING YOU BACK IN THE AIR ISN'T UP TO ME.
ONE FLIGHT.

I SAID IT'S NOT UP TO ME.
LOOK, I'M GETTING OLD. BUSINESS HASN'T BEEN GREAT...
...I GOT AN OFFER I COULDN'T REFUSE LAST WEEK.

I'M SELLING TO FERRIS AIR.
FERRIS?! YOU CAN'T BE SERIOUS.
AFTER WHAT HE DID... HOW COULD YOU SELL TO FERRIS?
MR. ARDEN?

I HOPE I'M NOT INTERRUPTING.

I HAVE THE FINAL PAPERS.
MY FATHER WOULD HAVE BROUGHT THEM HIMSELF, BUT APPARENTLY HE'S GOLFING THE GAME OF HIS *LIFE* IN PEBBLE BEACH.

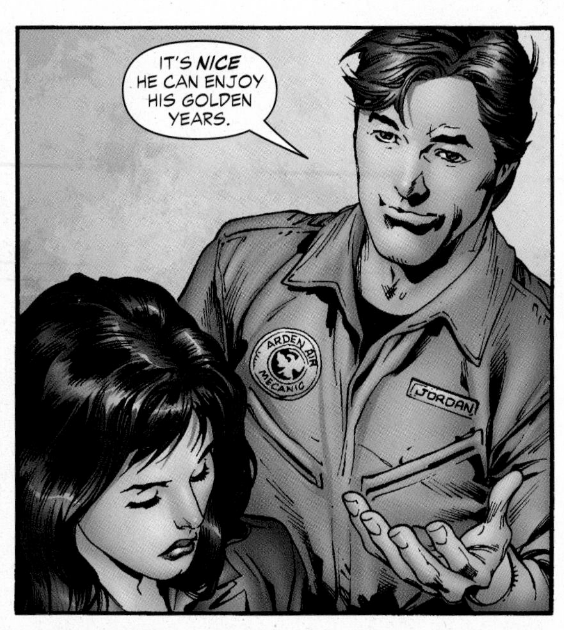
IT'S *NICE* HE CAN ENJOY HIS GOLDEN YEARS.
ARDEN AIR MECANIC
JORDAN

CAROL. THIS IS HAL--
JORDAN. OF COURSE. IT'S BEEN A LONG TIME.
CAROL'S FATHER RETIRED A FEW YEARS AGO. SHE'S COME OUT OF THE COCKPIT TO RUN FERRIS AIR.

YOU'RE A PILOT?
I *WAS.* I HAVE MORE IMPORTANT THINGS TO DO.

LIKE *NOW,* MR. JORDAN.

HE'S A PROBLEM.
THE DEAL WAS YOU KEEP HIM ON.

MY FATHER'S NOT GOING TO LIKE THIS.

DAMMIT, DAD.
ARDEN-AIR
MECHANIC

YOU CANNOT STOP "THE BLACKEST NIGHT," GREEN LANTERN. YOU CAN ONLY FACE IT.
LIKE YOUR OWN DEATH.
I AM NOT AFRAID OF DEATH, ATROCITUS.
BUT YOU ARE AFRAID.
WE HAVE SHARED OUR VISION OF YOUR RING FAILING YOU WHEN YOU NEEDED IT MOST.
NOW YOU FLY IN A SHIP. ARMED WITH WEAPONS.
I SIMPLY REMAIN CAUTIOUS.

YOUR FAITH IN YOUR POWER IS WEAKENING.
YOU'RE AFRAID TO RELY ON YOUR RING. YOU DON'T BELIEVE YOUR RING IS STRONG ENOUGH TO SAVE YOU.

YOUR WEAKNESS IN YOUR OWN WILLPOWER AND YOUR POWER RING--

--CARRIES THROUGH TO YOUR CONSTRUCTS.
YOU FEEL FEAR...
KRRAKK

...AND I FEEL FREEDOM!

THE IRONY OF IT ALL. IN THE MOMENT OF DEATH, YOUR RING DID NOT FAIL YOU, LANTERN.
YOU FAILED IT.

N-NO.
AAARRR!

FREEDOM!

GOODBYE, GREEN LANTERN.

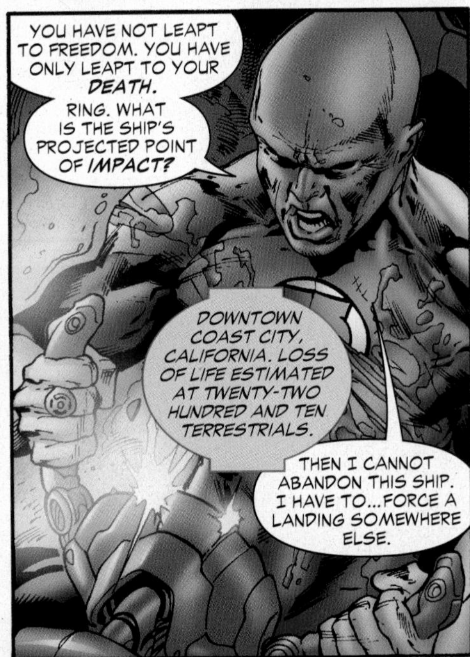
YOU HAVE NOT LEAPT TO FREEDOM. YOU HAVE ONLY LEAPT TO YOUR DEATH.
RING. WHAT IS THE SHIP'S PROJECTED POINT OF IMPACT?
DOWNTOWN COAST CITY, CALIFORNIA. LOSS OF LIFE ESTIMATED AT TWENTY-TWO HUNDRED AND TEN TERRESTRIALS.
THEN I CANNOT ABANDON THIS SHIP. I HAVE TO...FORCE A LANDING SOMEWHERE ELSE.

KAA-TANGG

BOOOOOMM

KAFF
...RING. PREPARE MESSAGE AND FILE INFORMATION FOR SINESTRO. HE MUST CONTINUE MY MISSION. IT IS NOT ONE FOR A ROOKIE...NNN...

SPACE SECTOR SCAN 2814 FOR REPLACEMENT SENTIENT INITIATED.

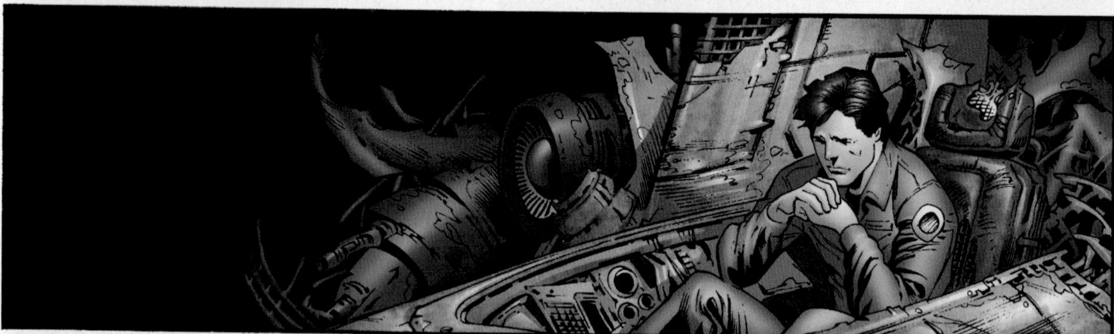

HAL JORDAN.
WHAT--?

YOU HAVE BEEN CHOSEN.
BOOOMMMM

I AM ABIN SUR. GREEN LANTERN OF YOUR SPACE SECTOR.
SPACE SECTOR 2814.
I AM DYING.
THE BRIGHTEST DAY BECOMES THE BLACKEST NIGHT.
TO SERVE IS A GREAT HONOR.
BESTOWED UPON YOU BY THE RING.

THE RING IS FUELED BY YOUR WILLPOWER.
THE GREATEST POWER IN THE UNIVERSE.
A UNIVERSE WHERE EVIL IS CONFRONTED BY THE GREEN LANTERN CORPS.
BY THE ORDER OF THE GUARDIANS.
JORDAN

THE RING WILL MAKE YOUR THOUGHTS AND WISHES A REALITY.
THE GREEN LANTERN'S LIGHT MUST BE RECHARGED WITH THE POWER BATTERY.
BUT THERE IS A FLAW IN THE BATTERY, AN IMPURITY LOCATED WITHIN YOUR VISUAL SPECTRUM.
THE POWER IS INEFFECTUAL AGAINST YELLOW.

YOU HAVE BEEN CHOSEN FOR ONE REASON.
AMONG MANY OTHERS.
YOU ARE A MAN WHO CAN OVERCOME GREAT FEAR.

HAL JORDAN OF EARTH.

DO YOU ACCEPT THIS DUTY?

I WAS DISORIENTED. THE LIGHT BLINDED MY EYES.
THE SOUNDS ECHOED IN THE CRAFT.
IF I'M NOT DREAMING--
--ABSOLUTELY.

AN EARTHMAN... heh...
...I NEVER THOUGHT I'D LIVE TO SEE THE DAY...
HE EXHALED ONE LAST TIME. AND I HEARD HIS FINAL WORD.

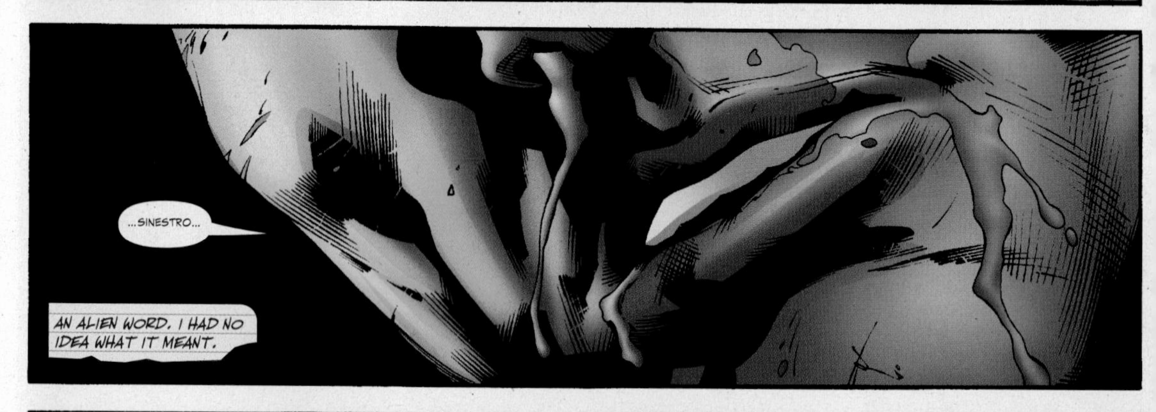
...SINESTRO...
AN ALIEN WORD. I HAD NO IDEA WHAT IT MEANT.

I HAD NO IDEA WHAT ANY OF THIS MEANT.
HAL JORDAN OF EARTH.
YOU HAVE THE ABILITY TO OVERCOME GREAT FEAR.

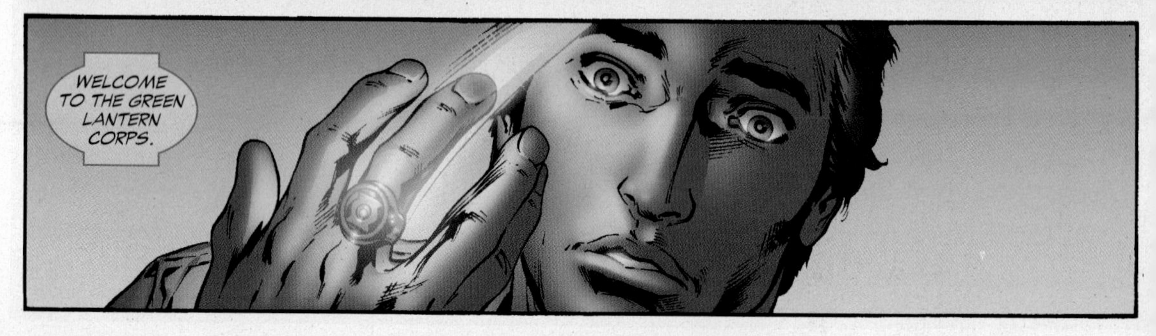
WELCOME TO THE GREEN LANTERN CORPS.

WHAT--?

GREEN LIGHT GRAFTED OVER MY BODY. IT WAS HOT.
FWOOOSHH

BUT THE BLACK WAS AS COLD AS ICE.

I NEED SOME AIR. GOTTA GET OUT.
WILLPOWER RECOGNIZED. RING ONLINE.
WHO IS THAT? WHO'S TALK--?
ORDERS ACCEPTED.
IS THAT THE RING?
AFFIRMATIVE.

BOOOMMM

HOLY #?$%!
HOLY #?$%!
HOLY #?$%!

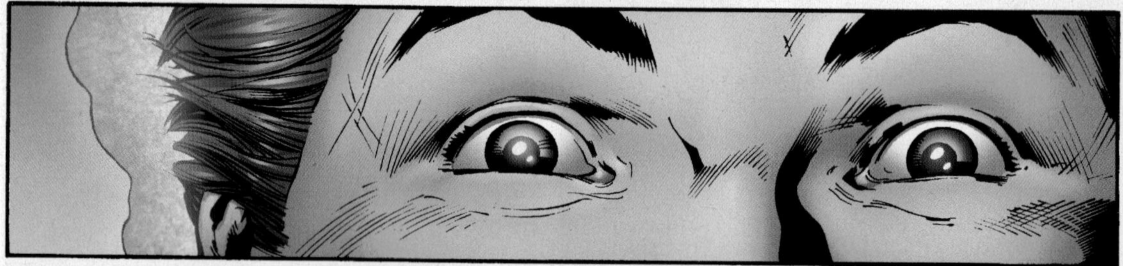

THERE WAS NO RUMBLING OF ANY ENGINE.
NO STICK TO PULL ON.
NO TOWER TO GET PERMISSION FROM.

IT WAS JUST ME.

ME AND THE RING.

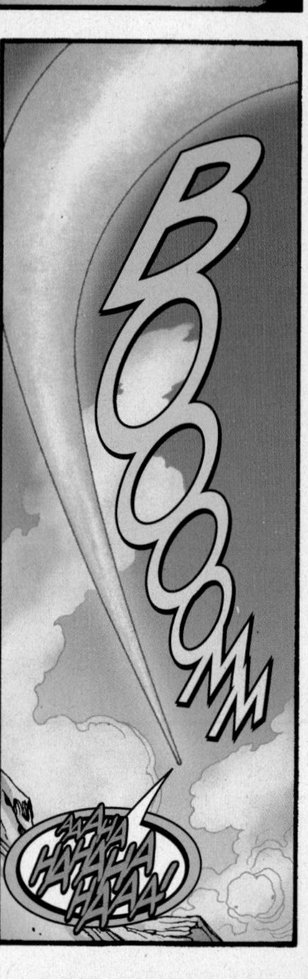
BOOOOOM
HAHAHAHAHAHAAA!

BOOMM
...YOU ARE CLEAR TO OPEN ENGINE FOUR, LAMINSKI.

LAMINSKI? DO YOU COPY?
YEAH, YEAH. I COPY THAT, TOWER.
YOU HEARD THE NEWS, RIGHT? FERRIS AIR BOUGHT ARDEN OUT. CARL FERRIS--
CARL FERRIS HAS BEEN RETIRED FOR YEARS. HE'S GOT THAT SWEET LITTLE PIECE OF MEAT HE CALLS A DAUGHTER RUNNING HIS AIRFIELDS.
WITHIN A WEEK, I'LL BE TEACHIN' HER A NEW MEANING FOR THE TERM "LANDING STRIP--"

BOM

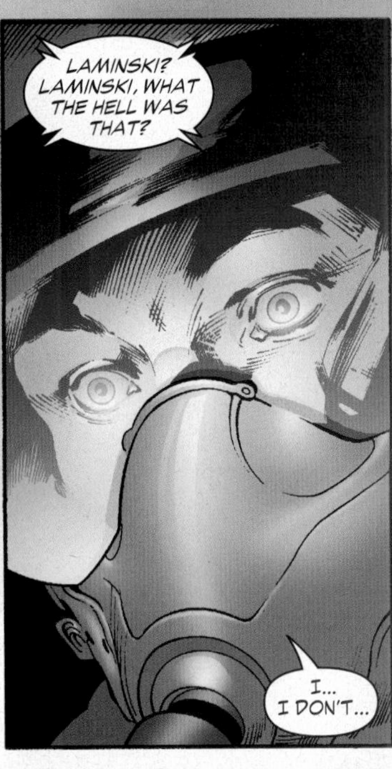
LAMINSKI? LAMINSKI, WHAT THE HELL WAS THAT?
I... I DON'T...

TEN TIMES THE PILOT.
YOU'RE LOSING CONTROL! LAMINSKI?!

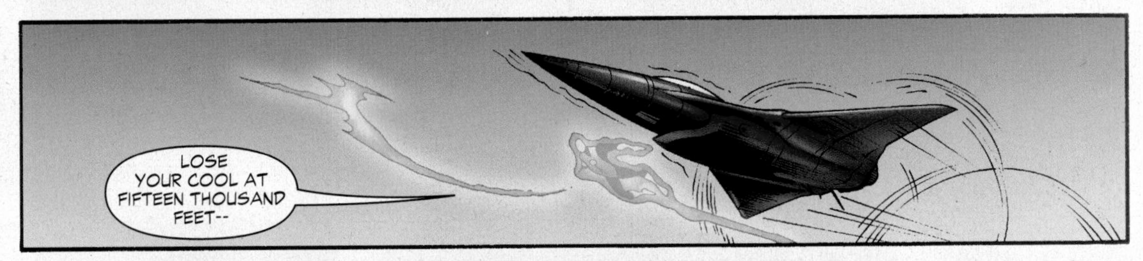
LOSE YOUR COOL AT FIFTEEN THOUSAND FEET--

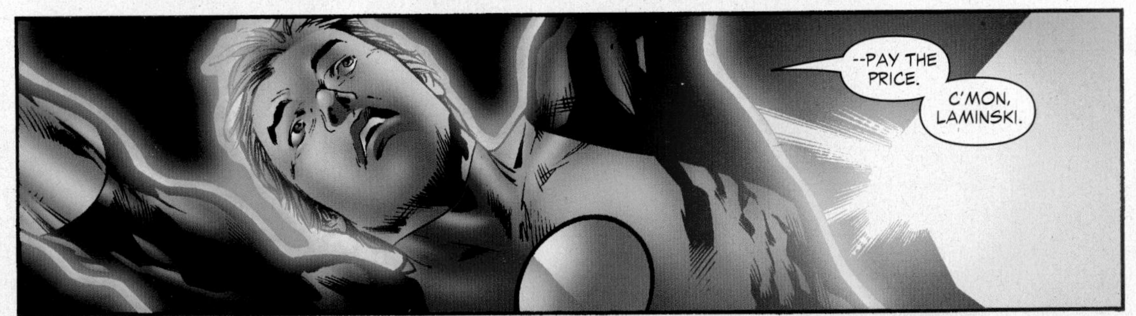
--PAY THE PRICE.
C'MON, LAMINSKI.

NO FEAR.

STEADY.
STEADY NOW.

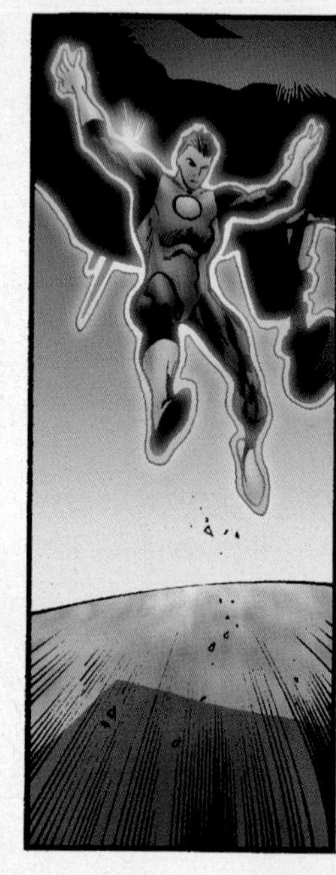

WHAT THE HELL HAPPENED, TOM?
I SAW SOMETHING GLOWING, MR. ARDEN. SOMETHING **GREEN.**

OW.
SENTIENTS APPROACHING.

CONCEALING IDENTITY.
Hnn.

STOP ***DOING*** THAT.

WHOA.

Um. HI.
YOUR PILOT MIGHT, uh, NEED SOME MEDICAL ATTENTION. I THINK I HEARD HIM THROW UP.

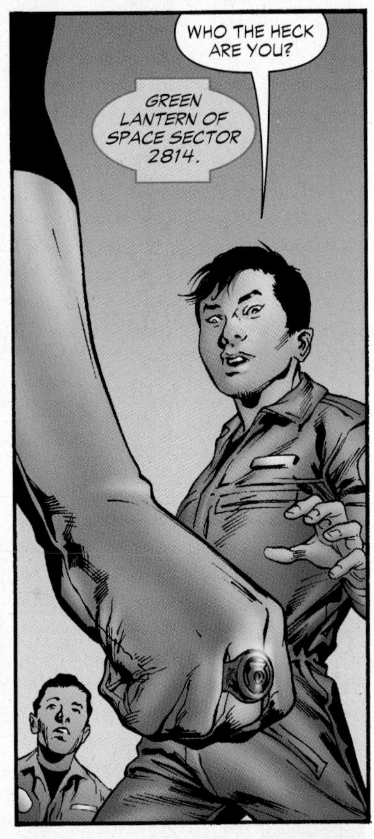
WHO THE HECK ARE YOU?
GREEN LANTERN OF SPACE SECTOR 2814.

GREEN... LANTERN?
WHAT'S A "GREEN LANTERN"?

KLUK

I'M CURIOUS WHAT A "GREEN LANTERN" IS MYSELF, CAROL.

THE NAME'S **HECTOR HAMMOND.**
YOU'RE NOT TRYING TO STEAL MY ***GIRL***--
--ARE YOU, SUPER-HERO?

SECRET ORIGIN
BOOK THREE

YOU'RE NOT TRYING TO STEAL MY GIRL, ARE YOU, SUPER-HERO?
CAROL HADN'T LOOKED UP FROM HER ACCOUNTING BOOKS IN YEARS.
SHE'D FORGOTTEN WHY SHE EVER DID.
Ah-HEM.

A LIFE TURNED UPSIDE DOWN.
I'M SURE MISS FERRIS APPRECIATES THE CATCH, BUT YOU CAN LET GO OF HER NOW.
RIGHT.
RIGHT.
A DYING ALIEN.

A WISHING RING.
THE GLOW OF THE UNIFORM KEPT THEM BLINDED ENOUGH. THEY DIDN'T RECOGNIZE ME BEHIND THE MASK.

AT LEAST, MOST OF THEM.
WHERE'D THOSE GIANT GREEN HANDS THAT WERE HOLDING THE PLANE GO? HOW'D YOU DO THAT?
CONSTRUCT MANIFESTATION TRIGGERED BY FORCE OF WILL.
WILL YOU SHUT UP?!
SILENT MODE ACTIVATED.

YOU ACT AS IF YOU BARELY KNOW WHAT'S HAPPENING YOURSELF.
I'M A SCIENTIST. I SPECIALIZE IN ASTROPHYSICS, ALTERNATIVE FUEL SOURCES AND THEORETICAL FUTURE-SCIENCE.
PERHAPS I CAN BE OF ASSISTANCE.
TRUTHFULLY, I DIDN'T KNOW WHAT I WAS DOING.

BUT I'D FIGURE IT OUT MYSELF.
NO, THANKS.
THAT'S WHAT I ALWAYS DID.

WHO IS HE?
WHERE'D HE COME FROM?
ARE YOU ALL RIGHT, CAROL?
CAROL.
I APPRECIATE YOUR CONCERN, DR. HAMMOND, BUT ONE DINNER DOES NOT MAKE ME "YOUR GIRL."
YOU'RE AN EMPLOYEE.

AND I'VE MADE IT CRYSTAL CLEAR. I DON'T DATE EMPLOYEES.

I'M NOT AN EMPLOYEE. I'M A CONSULTANT.
YOU CAN'T TREAT ME LIKE YOU DO EVERYONE ELSE. FERRIS AIR ISN'T THE ONLY COMPANY I WORK--
VEETVEET

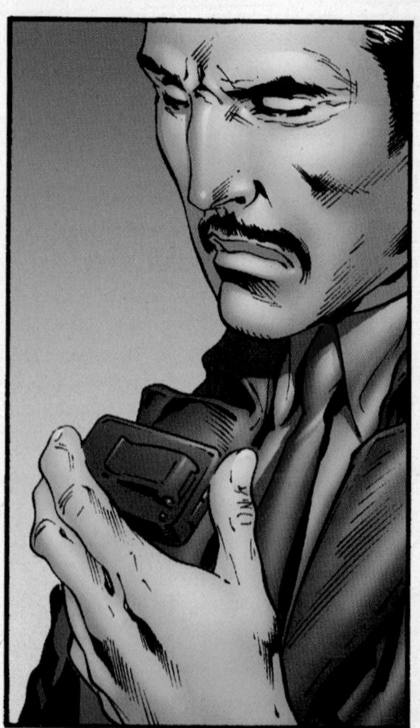

TELL YOUR FATHER "HELLO."
WHO WAS HE?

I ASKED THE SAME QUESTIONS EVERYONE AT FERRIS DID.

ABOUT THIS ALIEN.
HE WAS OBVIOUSLY SOME KIND OF SOLDIER OR OFFICER.

I WASN'T GOING TO LEAVE HIM OUT IN THE OPEN.

HE DESERVED BETTER THAN THAT.
NO MATTER WHO HE WAS.

THE GREEN LANTERN? IS THAT WHAT THIS IS?
RING? RING, YOU CAN TALK NOW.

THIS IS YOUR POWER BATTERY.
POWER BATTERY? WHAT'S A POWER BATTER--

HEY!

A GREEN LANTERN'S POWER BATTERY IS THEIR POWER RING'S CHARGING STATION. RECHARGING REQUIRED APPROXIMATELY EVERY TWENTY-FOUR TERRESTRIAL HOURS.
LET GO, DAMMIT!
INCORRECT OATH.
KLANK
POWER LEVELS 100%.

GREEN LANTERN OF SPACE SECTOR 2814.
YOU WILL REPORT TO OA FOR TRAINING IMMEDIATELY.
WHAT?

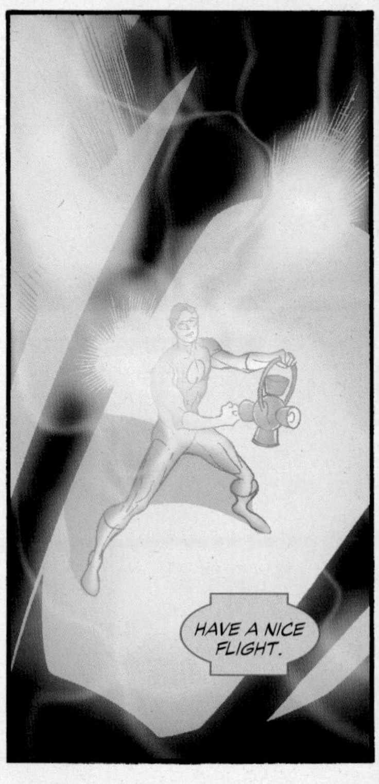
HAVE A NICE FLIGHT.

BOOOOOM
DESCENDING FROM HYPERSPACE.
UNIVERSAL TRANSLATOR ON.
HEY!

I HEARD STRANGE SOUNDS AS THE LIGHT HIT MY EYES.
THEY WERE FILTERED THROUGH THE RING, CREATING AN ECHO OF A LANGUAGE I COULD UNDERSTAND.
WATCH WHERE YOU'RE FLYING, $#?%!
I FELT RIGHT AT HOME.

WHERE THE HELL AM I?
THE PLANET OA. CENTRAL PRECINCT OF THE GREEN LANTERN CORPS.
AND HOME TO THE GUARDIANS OF THE UNIVERSE-- IMMORTAL WATCHERS AND PROTECTORS OF ALL.
ABIN?

DISENGAGING AUTOPILOT.
WAIT. WHY DID YOU BRING ME HERE?
WHAT AM I SUPPOSED TO DO NOW?
HELLO?!
TUTORIAL OFF.

IS THAT A HUMAN?
A HUMAN GREEN LANTERN?
WHAT'S A HUMAN?

THAT'S NO WAY TA TREAT YOUR BATTERY.

NICE LANDIN', *POOZER.*
NAME'S **KILOWOG.**
WELCOME TA RINGSLINGIN' 101. OR AS KE'HAAN AND I LIKE TO CALL IT--

--THE **WORST** DAY A' YOUR **WORTHLESS LIFE!**

OH, I GET IT.
THIS IS *BOOT CAMP.*

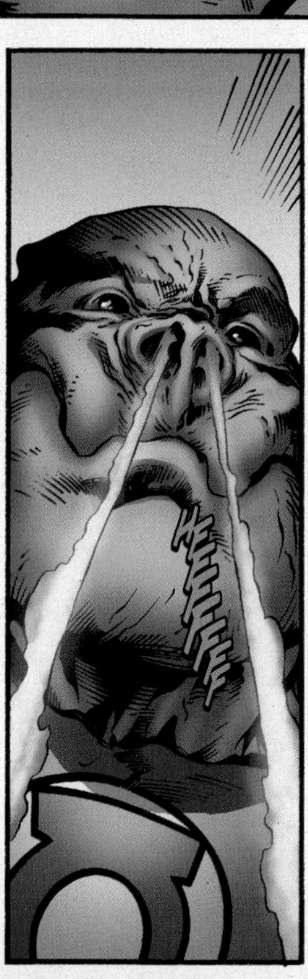

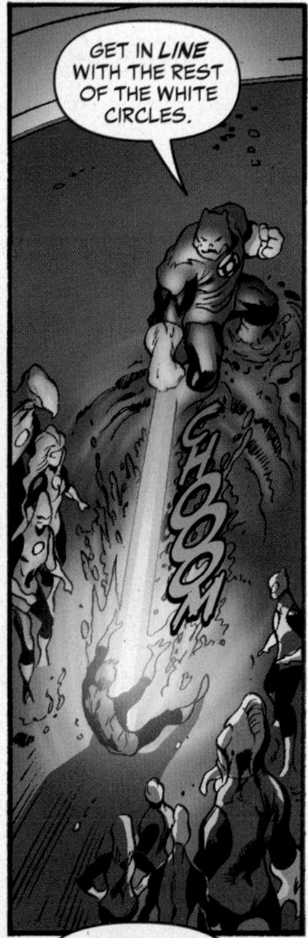
GET IN *LINE* WITH THE REST OF THE WHITE CIRCLES.
CHOOOM

IT'S WHERE YOU PRIMORDIAL QUADRUPEDS *BELONG.*
YOU WANNA BOX?

LET'S BOX.

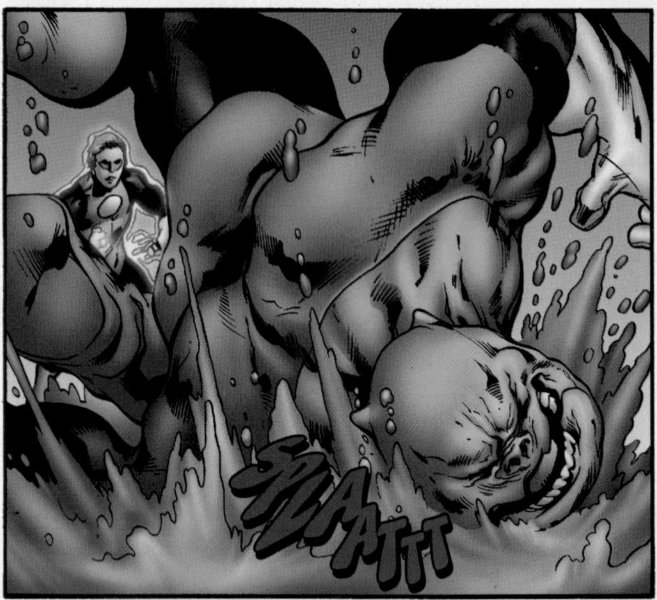
SMAATTT

YOU REALLY SHOULDN'T HAVE DONE THAT.
WHY NOT?

BECAUSE I'VE BEEN LOOKIN' ALL DAY FOR SOMEBODY TA MAKE AN EXAMPLE OUTTA!

THEY WERE TRACKING IT WHEN IT FLEW PAST MARS.

BUT IT WASN'T UNTIL IT *TURNED* TOWARD EARTH THAT IT WAS RED FLAGGED.
SOMETHING BROKE OFF WHEN IT ENTERED THE ATMOSPHERE. RIGHT ABOVE BIG BEAR, CALIFORNIA.
FORT ROCK'S SENT A UNIT TO INVESTIGATE THE SECOND CRASH SITE. WE'RE HANDLING THIS ONE.
WHAT IS IT, MAJOR STONE? A FALLEN SPY SATELLITE? A METEOR?

YOU'RE THE SCIENTIST THAT SPECIALIZES IN THE THEORETICAL, DR. HAMMOND.
YOU TELL US.
MY GOD...

"...WE'RE NOT ALONE."
SOMETHING LANDED HERE.
LOOKS LIKE IT SLID INTO THE WATER.

WE MIGHT NEED SOME S.E.A.L.S TO...HEY.

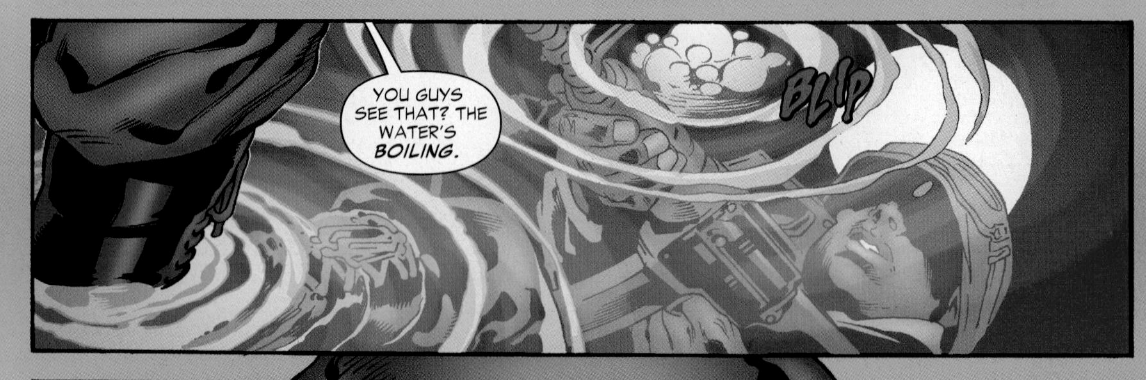
YOU GUYS SEE THAT? THE WATER'S BOILING.
BLIP

RRAAAARRRR!
DEATH WILL CLAIM YOU. YOU AND ALL THAT THE GREEN LANTERN CORPS RULE OVER.
SO SWEAR THE SURVIVORS OF SECTOR 666.

THE RING CAN MAKE WHATEVER TOOL YA NEED. JUST GOTTA PICTURE IT IN YOUR MIND. WILL IT TO LIFE.
FORCE FIELDS. ENERGY BEAMS.
EVERYONE SEE THAT?
YES, SIR.

YOU PRACTICE WELL, AHTIER. WHY DO YOU SPEAK SO LITTLE?
BECAUSE I FEAR MY DUTY, KE'HAAN.
GREEN LANTERNS BURN BRIGHT, BUT THEY BURN OUT QUICKLY.
IF THAT HUMAN CAN MAKE IT, SO CAN YOU.

THANKS FOR THE RIDE, BUT I'LL GET OFF HERE.

KKRSHH

YOU WILLED YOURSELF FREE, EARTHMAN...

...NOW TRY CATCHIN' THIS.

NnNGg

WHAT THE HELL HAPPENED?
WHAT DO YOU MEAN WHAT HAPPENED, HUMAN? IT WAS YELLOW.
EVERYONE IN THE UNIVERSE KNOWS A GREEN LANTERN'S POWER RING IS INEFFECTUAL AGAINST YELLOW.

HE DON'T KNOW NOTHIN' 'BOUT THE CORPS, CH'P. HE'S FROM EARTH.
ASK ME, KILOWOG, EARTH'S A BACKWARD WORLD BEST LEFT TO THEIR OWN.

WHY YELLOW?
WHAT?
WHY WOULD THESE RINGS NOT BE ABLE TO AFFECT ANYTHING YELLOW?

YOU DON'T ASK QUESTIONS IN THE CORPS. YOU DO YOUR DUTY.
I DON'T EVEN KNOW WHAT THAT "DUTY" IS.
"TO SERVE AND PROTECT YOUR RESPECTIVE SECTORS AND ALL LIFE WITHIN THEM."
NOW DON'T GET ALL PUFFY CHESTED AGAIN. NEXT TIME, I WON'T BE SO NICE.
KILOWOG.

LET ME SPEAK WITH THE EARTHMAN.
WHAT BUSINESS IS HE OF YOURS, TOMAR?

HE'S WEARING ABIN SUR'S RING.

MY NAME IS TOMAR-RE OF XUDAR. GREEN LANTERN OF SPACE SECTOR 2815.
BY ALL ACCOUNTS, I AM YOUR NEIGHBOR.
I'M HAL JORDAN.
ABIN SUR'S REPLACEMENT IN THE CORPS. MY RING IS UNABLE TO UNLOCK HIS LOG...HOW DID HE DIE?
HE CRASHED HIS SHIP IN THE DESERT.

HIS SHIP?
HE DIDN'T NEED THAT SHIP.

THEN WHY WAS HE FLYING ONE?
HE DID WHAT NO GREEN LANTERN SHOULD. HE ALLOWED HIMSELF TO FEEL FEAR.
AND IT HAPPENED BECAUSE ABIN SUR DISOBEYED THE GUARDIAN'S TERRITORIAL EDICT AND PURSUED AN ENEMY OUTSIDE OF HIS SECTOR.

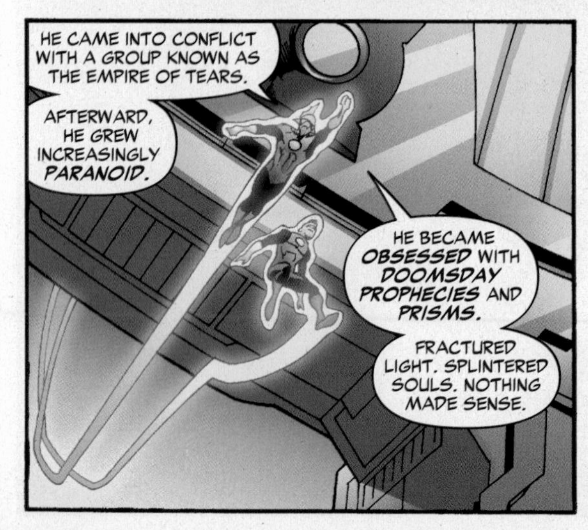
HE CAME INTO CONFLICT WITH A GROUP KNOWN AS THE EMPIRE OF TEARS.
AFTERWARD, HE GREW INCREASINGLY PARANOID.
HE BECAME OBSESSED WITH DOOMSDAY PROPHECIES AND PRISMS.
FRACTURED LIGHT. SPLINTERED SOULS. NOTHING MADE SENSE.

NOTHING MAKES SENSE TO ME RIGHT NOW.

THIS IS THE BOOK OF OA. IN IT-- TALES OF THE GREEN LANTERN CORPS.

ABIN SUR'S TALE IS NOW AMONG THEM. AN ENDING TRAGIC.
ONE DAY YOUR TALE WILL BE HERE TOO, AS WILL MINE.
A WORD OF ADVICE, SUCCESSOR.

IF YOU NEED HELP--
--ASK FOR IT.

THE SUN NEVER SET.
YER SUPPOSED TA FLY AROUND THEM, JORDAN, NOT THROUGH THEM!

I DIDN'T KNOW HOW LONG I GOT MY ASS HANDED TO ME.
I'LL DO IT.
YOU WON'T DO IT.
IT'S JUST A COLOR.

DAYS.
YOU MISHANDLE YOUR POWER BATTERY AGAIN, HAL JORDAN, AND SHORM WILL MISHANDLE YOU.
UNDERSTOOD, SALAAK.

YOU STILL GOT CRACKS IN YOUR CONSTRUCTS, JORDAN--
--BUT IT AIN'T BAD.
A WEEK?

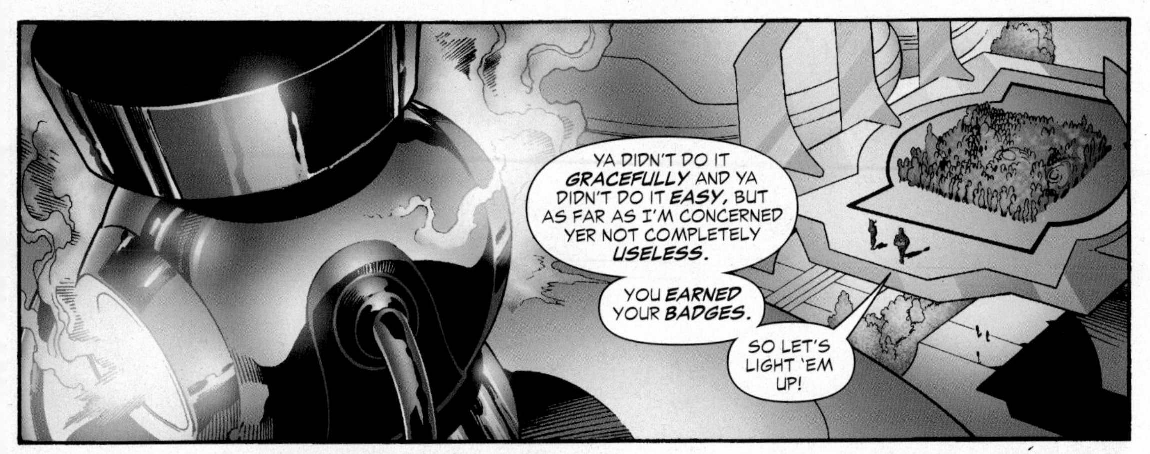
YA DIDN'T DO IT GRACEFULLY AND YA DIDN'T DO IT EASY, BUT AS FAR AS I'M CONCERNED YER NOT COMPLETELY USELESS.
YOU EARNED YOUR BADGES.
SO LET'S LIGHT 'EM UP!

IN BRIGHTEST DAY IN BLACKEST NIGHT
IN BRIGHTEST DAY... IN BLACKEST NIGHT

NO EVIL SHALL ESCAPE MY SIGHT
NO EVIL SHALL ESCAPE MY SIGHT

LET THOSE WHO WORSHIP EVIL'S MIGHT...
LET THOSE WHO WORSHIP EVIL'S MIGHT

BEWARE MY POWER-- GREEN LANTERN'S LIGHT!
BEWARE MY POWER-- GREEN LANTERN'S LIGHT!

WHY WAS I NOT NOTIFIED IMMEDIATELY, GUARDIAN?
YOU WERE ENGAGED IN BATTLE WITH THE MANHUNTERS. WE DID NOT WANT YOUR FOCUS DISRUPTED.
RIDICULOUS. WHEN HAS MY FOCUS **EVER** BEEN DISRUPTED?
IT IS TRUE. YOUR RECORD IS FAR SUPERIOR TO THAT OF YOUR FELLOW OFFICERS. YOUR SECTOR IS NEARLY CLEAN OF THE CHAOS THAT ONCE CLAIMED IT.
YOU HAVE BEEN CALLED THE "GREATEST" BY MANY.

...HAVE I?
THAT IS WHY I ASK YOU TO VENTURE TO EARTH WHERE YOU WILL CONTACT ABIN SUR'S REPLACEMENT AND INVESTIGATE THE CIRCUMSTANCES INVOLVING HIS DEATH.
WHAT OF PROPER PROTOCOL? SALAAK HAS NOT DOWNLOADED THE OFFICIAL MISSION TO MY RING, GUARDIAN.
THIS MISSION WILL STAY BETWEEN **US.** AND YOU CAN CALL ME GANTHET.

GANTHET? WHY HAVE YOU TAKEN A NAME WHEN NO **OTHER** GUARDIANS HAVE?
SO THAT YOU **KNOW** ME.
GREEN LANTERNS **PARTNERING** UP? THIS GOES AGAINST YOUR **TERRITORIAL EDICT.**
I AM ASKING YOU TO BREAK THAT EDICT--
--FOR YOUR MENTOR AND FRIEND.
WELL THEN, **GANTHET...**

...I AM ON MY WAY TO EARTH.

HIGHBALL

SECRET ORIGIN

BOOK FOUR

EDWARDS AIR FORCE BASE.
HANGAR 44.
HAS ANYONE SEEN DR. HAMMOND?
...THIS IS THE SIXTH MESSAGE I'VE LEFT, CAROL.
YOU CALL ME BACK AND WE CAN SMOOTH ALL OF THIS TENSION OUT OVER DINNER--
--OR YOU CAN CONSIDER MY ENDORSEMENT OF FERRIS AIR'S AERONAUTICS VOIDED. ON TOP OF EVERYTHING ELSE THAT'S HAPPENED THIS WEEK, I'M SURE YOU AND YOUR FATHER DON'T NEED THAT.
DR. HAMMOND.
WHAT IS IT?
IT TOOK US A FEW DAYS, BUT WE'VE FINALLY DISASSEMBLED THE ALIEN CRAFT'S THRUSTERS.
WHAT?
WE'VE DISASSEMBLED THE THRUSTERS. WE CAN REACH THE FUEL CHAMBERS, BUT WE'RE HESITANT ABOUT OPENING--
HESITANT? USE YOUR COMMON SENSE.
YOUR HELMET, DR. HAMMOND--
DO YOU HEAR THAT? THE FUEL CHAMBER'S EMPTY.
LIKE YOUR HEADS.
KONGG KONGG
FSSSSSS
YOU SEE?
THERE'S NOTHING TO BE AFRAID OF.

CLOSE THE DOOR!
WHAT IS IT?
THE SHIP'S FUEL ISN'T A *LIQUID!* IT'S POWERED BY SOME KIND OF *ROCK!*
LOOKS LIKE A METEOR.
GET HAMMOND CLEAR!

HE'S GOING INTO CONVULSIONS!
NnNNnnNn!

HAMMOND'S SO *CREEPY*.
WH-WHAT DID YOU SAY?

MEDIC! WE NEED A *MEDIC!*
LOOKS LIKE HE'S ALL RIGHT. TOO BAD.
GOD, I HOPE HE'S ALL RIGHT.
THAT MUSTACHE MAKES HIM LOOK LIKE A PEDOPHILE.
WHAT'S WRONG WITH HIS HEAD?
HECTOR HAMMOND IS A LOSER.

TERRIBLE TASTE IN SUITS.
HE'S ALWAYS CALLING CAROL FERRIS. LIKE SOME KIND OF STALKER.
SHUT UP.
HIS BREATH IS TERRIBLE.

SHUT UP!

WHAT THE HELL DID HE DO?
I DID NOT SIGN UP FOR THIS!
WE SHOULD JUST SHOOT THIS #$%&!
STAY WHERE YOU ARE.

PENNY FOR YOUR THOUGHTS?

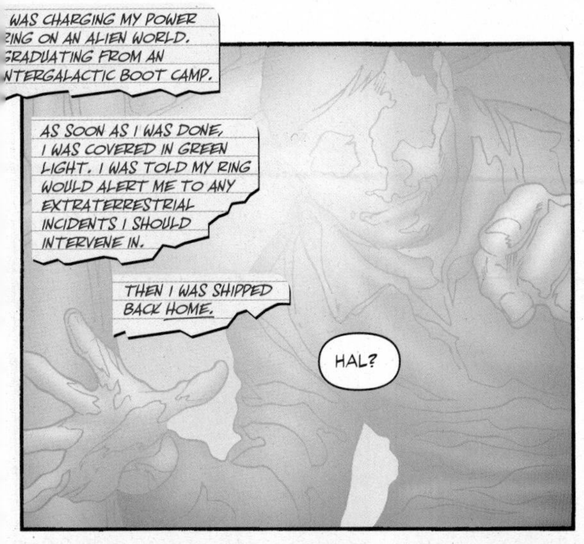
WAS CHARGING MY POWER
RING ON AN ALIEN WORLD.
GRADUATING FROM AN
INTERGALACTIC BOOT CAMP.
AS SOON AS I WAS DONE, I WAS COVERED IN GREEN LIGHT. I WAS TOLD MY RING WOULD ALERT ME TO ANY EXTRATERRESTRIAL INCIDENTS I SHOULD INTERVENE IN.
THEN I WAS SHIPPED BACK HOME.
HAL?

TOM?
I CAN'T BELIEVE IT! YOU'RE THE ***GREEN LANTERN!***
ANY LIFE OUTSIDE THE CORPS WASN'T TAKEN INTO CONSIDERATION.

THE...GREEN LANTERN?
WHAT ARE YOU, *uh,* TALKING ABOUT?
WELL, YOU'RE WEARING A GLOWING GREEN ***RING.***
FERRIS AIR

AND THERE'S ***THIS.***

WHAT DO YOU MEAN YOU'RE NOT A SUPER-HERO?
YOU CAUGHT LAMINSKI'S PLANE LAST WEEK!
ANYONE ELSE WOULD'VE DONE THE SAME IF THEY COULD.
EVEN IF HE IS A JERK.

WELL, YOU'RE NOT GONNA HAVE TO WORRY ABOUT HIM ANYMORE.
I'M NOT SUPPOSED TO USE THE RING TO SORT OUT PERSONAL PROBLEMS, TOM.
NO, I MEAN THE WALKOUT.

WHAT WALKOUT?
KLANG

SEE ALL THE EMPTY LOCKERS?
ONCE WORD SPREAD THAT CAROL "LADY" FERRIS WAS TAKING THE REINS FROM MR. ARDEN, NO ONE WAS PARTICULARLY EXCITED.
AND AFTER HER FATHER DIDN'T SHOW FOR THE BIG COMPANY SPEECH, SHE HAD TO GIVE IT HERSELF--

--AFTERWARDS JUST ABOUT EVERYONE QUIT.

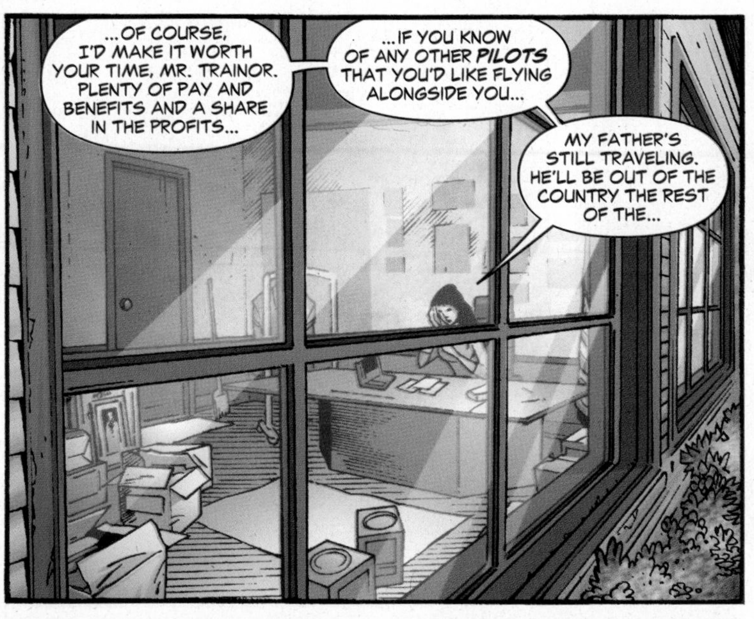
...OF COURSE, I'D MAKE IT WORTH YOUR TIME, MR. TRAINOR. PLENTY OF PAY AND BENEFITS AND A SHARE IN THE PROFITS...
...IF YOU KNOW OF ANY OTHER *PILOTS* THAT YOU'D LIKE FLYING ALONGSIDE YOU...
MY FATHER'S STILL TRAVELING. HE'LL BE OUT OF THE COUNTRY THE REST OF THE...

YES, OF COURSE, HE WOULD'VE MADE THE CALL HIMSELF IF HE COULD, BUT...
MR. TRAINOR, LISTEN TO ME. THIS IS THE OPPORTUNITY OF A... MR. TRAINOR?
...LARRY?

FRAGILE

NOK NOK

YES?

MISS FERRIS.
MR. JORDAN? WHAT ARE YOU DOING HERE?
I JUST WANTED TO THROW IN MY RESIGNATION ALONG WITH THE REST.

YOU HAVEN'T SHOWN YOUR FACE HERE ALL WEEK. I ASSUMED YOU ALREADY HAD.
YOU ASSUMED RIGHT. I GUESS I WANTED TO MAKE IT OFFICIAL.
AND IF YOUR FATHER WAS HERE--

WHAT?
WHAT WOULD YOU DO IF MY FATHER WAS HERE?

I'D TELL HIM WHAT I'VE BEEN WANTING TO FOR YEARS.
I'D TELL HIM EVERYTHING MY MOTHER BEGGED ME NOT TO.

YOU KNOW WHAT, JORDAN? LET'S MAKE THIS DAY EVEN BETTER THAN IT HAS BEEN.
TELL ME.

YOUR FATHER PUT MINE IN A DEATH TRAP!
HE SAVED A FEW BUCKS AND HE SENT HIM OFF IN A PLANE THAT NEVER HAD A CHANCE AT LANDING.

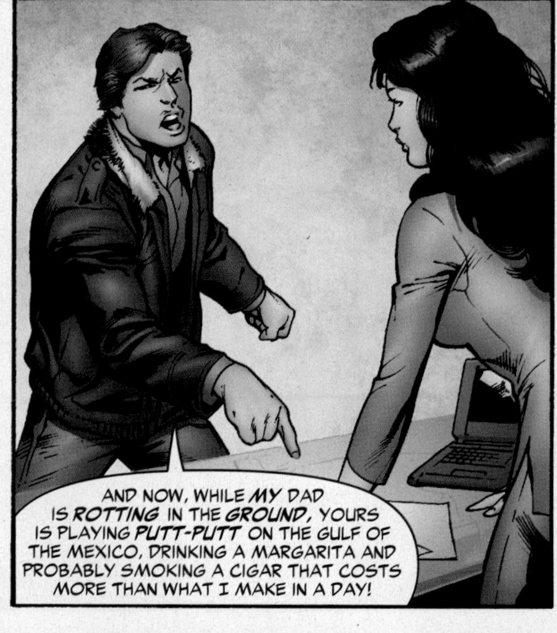
AND NOW, WHILE MY DAD IS ROTTING IN THE GROUND, YOURS IS PLAYING PUTT-PUTT ON THE GULF OF THE MEXICO, DRINKING A MARGARITA AND PROBABLY SMOKING A CIGAR THAT COSTS MORE THAN WHAT I MAKE IN A DAY!

YOU DON'T MAKE ANYTHING, JORDAN. YOU JUST QUIT, REMEMBER?
NOW IS THAT ALL YOU'VE GOT TO BARK ABOUT?

FORGET IT, "LADY" FERRIS. I'LL SAVE THE REST FOR HIM WHEN HE'S BACK FROM HIS EXTENDED HOLIDAY.

DO YOU WANT TO FLY AGAIN?

WHAT?

DO YOU WANT TO FLY AGAIN?
YES.
BUT NOT HERE.
THEN WHERE?

WHO'S GOING TO HIRE YOU?
AFTER EVERYTHING YOU'VE DONE, WHO'S GOING TO TAKE THAT RISK?

I DIDN'T NEED A PLANE TO FLY ANYMORE.
THE RING MADE IT EASY.

THE RING MADE IT TOO EASY.

PLEASE, HAL.
I NEED A PILOT. AND YOU NEED A PLANE.
FOR A SPLIT SECOND, I DIDN'T SEE THE SHARK I THOUGHT SHE WAS. I SAW THE LITTLE GIRL I'D MET ALL THAT TIME AGO.
SHE CRIED LOUDER THAN I DID WHEN MY FATHER'S PLANE CRASHED.
SOMEHOW I'D FORGOTTEN THAT.

WITH BLOOD AND RAGE OF CRIMSON RED

RIPPED FROM A CORPSE SO FRESHLY DEAD

TOGETHER WITH OUR HELLISH HATE

IT FELT GOOD TO FLY.
BUT IN THE BACK OF MY HEAD, I KNEW I WAS FLYING FOR THE WRONG PERSON.

I CONVINCED MYSELF I WAS ONLY STAYING UNTIL CARL FERRIS CAME BACK.
UNTIL I FINALLY GOT AN ANSWER TO THE QUESTION I'VE ASKED MYSELF A MILLION TIMES OVER.
HOW COULD HE LIVE THE WAY HE DOES AFTER WHAT HAPPENED?
HOW COULD HE SHIRK THE RESPONSIBILITY?

I TRIED TO STAY ANGRY IN THE AIR, BUT IT WAS HARD.
THE OPEN SKY INVITING ME BACK IN. AND CAROL FERRIS...
...WHY COULDN'T I STOP THINKING ABOUT HER?

CAROL.
FERRIS WANTS THIS ONE PRECISE, JORDAN. WE'RE ABOUT ROBUST TRAJECTORY TRACKING TODAY, NOT SPLIT-S MANEUVERS.
I WAS JUST LOOSENING UP.

WHAT HAPPENED TO THAT GIRL?
I DON'T KNOW IF THIS IS SUCH A GOOD IDEA, MISS FERRIS.
HE'S WANDERING ALL OVER THE PLACE. IF HE STARTS SOME OF HIS HOTDOGGING--
THIS IS HIS LAST CHANCE.

HE CAN'T SCREW IT UP.

VROOOM
WHAT IS THAT IMBECILE DOING?

FLYING WITHOUT HIS POWER RING.
WITHOUT HIS...? RING. LOCATE HIS POWER RING.

"THIS MAVERICK NEEDS A LESSON IN RESPONSIBILITY.
"BRING HIS RING TO ME."
WHOA!

HEY.
I'VE GOT SOMETHING AT TWELVE O'CLOCK. THOUGHT I WAS ALONE UP HERE.
NOTHING ON OUR SCREEN. ARE YOU SURE?
VEEP VEEP VEEP

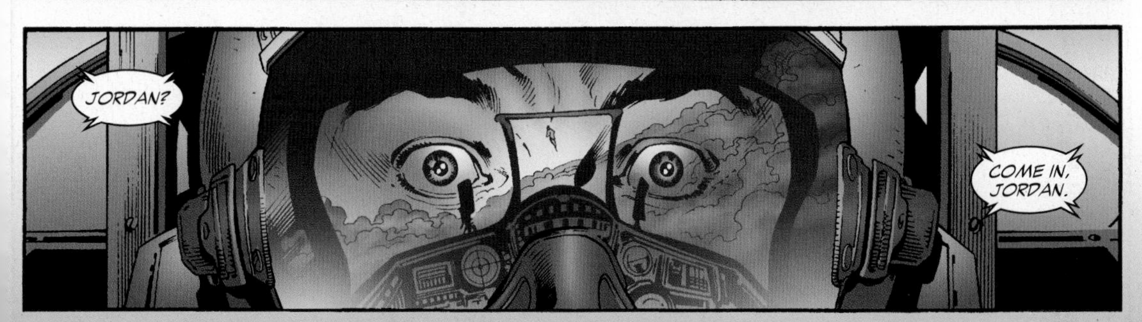
JORDAN?
COME IN, JORDAN.

GREEN LANTERN OF SECTOR 2814.
YOU ARE *WASTING* TIME.

WHAT ARE YOU DOING?!
WHO THE HELL ARE YOU?
I AM SINESTRO.
GREEN LANTERN OF SECTOR 1417.
IS THAT SUPPOSED TO IMPRESS ME?
I WOULDN'T REMEMBER UNTIL LATER, "SINESTRO" WAS ABIN SUR'S LAST WORD.

I NEVER THOUGHT IT WAS A NAME.
Hr.
RING?
SECTOR 1417. THE MOST ORDERLY SECTOR IN ALL THE UNIVERSE.
AND I AM THE GREATEST GREEN LANTERN.

WHAT THE HELL HAPPENED UP THERE?
WE DON'T KNOW, MISS FERRIS.
HE JUST DISAPPEARED. AND WE CAN'T MAKE CONTACT.

...WHO'S GOING TO SHELL OUT THE TWENTY MILLION DOLLARS FOR THAT JET?
I DON'T SEE ANY POCKETS.
YOUR TERRESTRIAL AFFAIRS SHOULD BE OF LITTLE CONCERN, EARTHMAN. YOU ARE IN THE PRESENCE OF A VETERAN.

NEVER QUESTION A SUPERIOR OFFICER.
NEVER CHALLENGE THOSE MORE POWERFUL THAN YOU.

Um... YEAH.
THAT'S NOT GONNA WORK FOR ME.

DO YOU HAVE ANY IDEA WHAT YOU JUST DID? WHAT YOU JUST COST ME?
RING. CAN YOU REBUILD THE PLANE?

THE QUESTION SHOULDN'T BE POSED TO YOUR RING, IT SHOULD BE POSED TO YOU.
WHAT DOES KILOWOG TEACH YOU WHITE CIRCLES THESE DAYS?
HE TAUGHT ME THAT MY DUTY WAS TO LOCATE ANY ALIENS CAUSING TROUBLE AND KICK THEM OFF PLANET.

YOUR CONSTRUCTS ARE WEAK.

THEY'RE LACED WITH ANGER.
AND ALTHOUGH THE GUARDIANS BELIEVE FEAR CREATES CRACKS IN OUR WILLPOWER--
--ANGER WILL DISTORT IT.

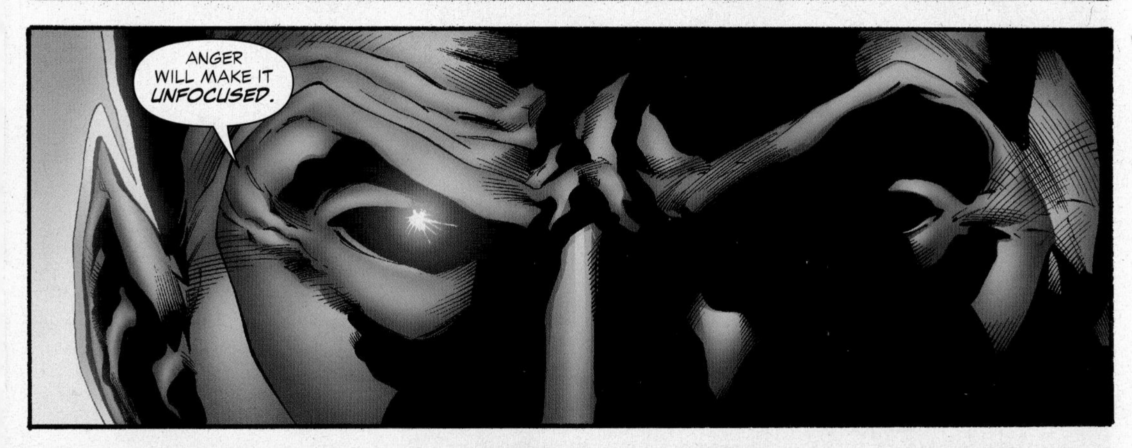
ANGER WILL MAKE IT UNFOCUSED.

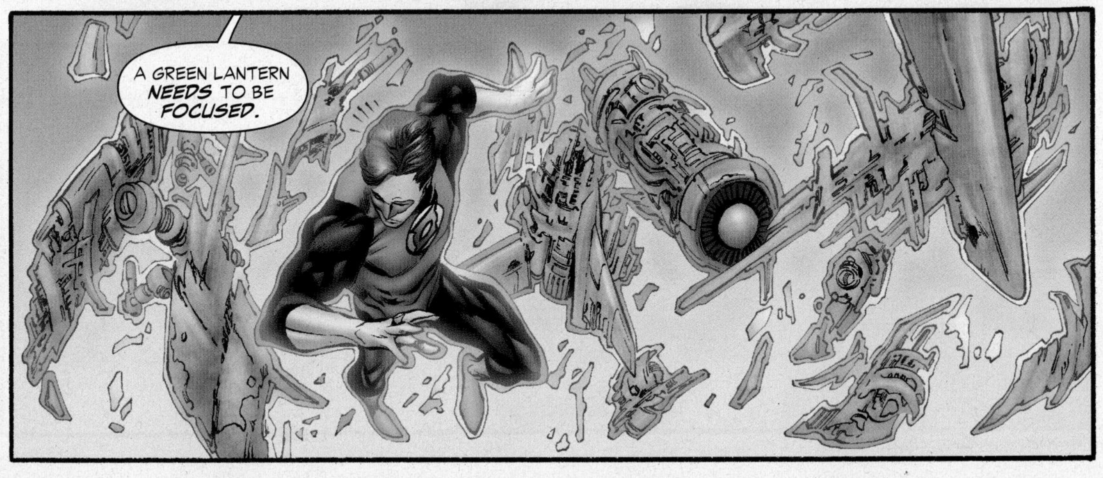
A GREEN LANTERN NEEDS TO BE FOCUSED.

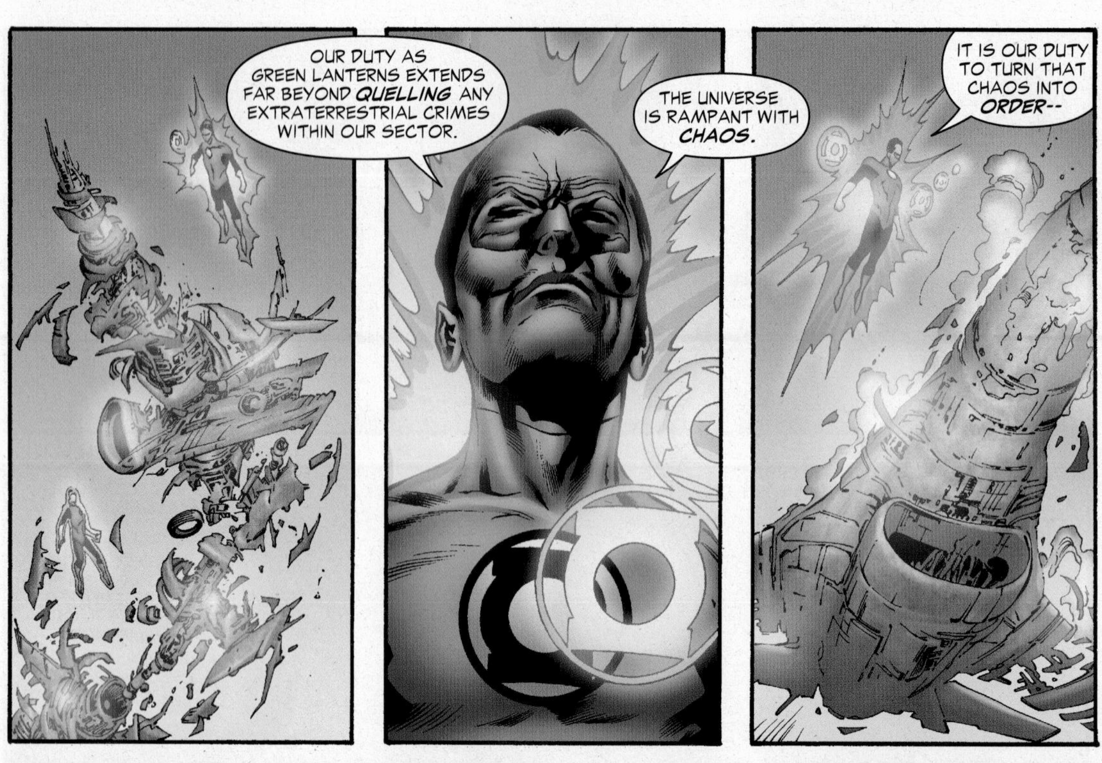
OUR DUTY AS GREEN LANTERNS EXTENDS FAR BEYOND QUELLING ANY EXTRATERRESTRIAL CRIMES WITHIN OUR SECTOR.
THE UNIVERSE IS RAMPANT WITH CHAOS.
IT IS OUR DUTY TO TURN THAT CHAOS INTO ORDER--

--AND MAINTAIN IT.

HOW DID YOU...?

I NEED TO GO.
GO? GO WHERE?
BACK TO MY REAL JOB.
YOU NEED MORE TRAINING, ROOKIE.

WHAT THE HELL ARE YOU DOING HERE ANYWAY? TOMAR-RE TOLD ME ALL OF US ARE SUPPOSED TO STAY IN OUR OWN SECTOR.
YES, THE GUARDIANS' TERRITORIAL EDICT DISSUADES FRATERNIZING AMONG THE CORPS.
BUT I HAVE MY ORDERS. AND THEY ARE FROM A MUCH HIGHER AUTHORITY THAN TOMAR-RE.

I'VE BEEN DISPATCHED TO THIS PRIMITIVE PLANET PLAGUED WITH POLITICAL BORDERS AND TERRESTRIAL WAR TO INVESTIGATE THE DEATH OF YOUR PREDECESSOR.

ABIN SUR CRASHED HIS SHIP IN THE CALIFORNIA DESERT.
WHY?
I DON'T KNOW. HE DIDN'T TELL--
GREEN LANTERN OF SPACE SECTOR 1417--MESSAGE FROM GREEN LANTERN 2814 WAITING.
WHAT? WHAT DID YOUR RING SAY?

I DON'T KNOW. MAYBE YOURS IS SCREWING WITH IT.
MESSAGE WAITING.

STAY OUT OF MY FLIGHT PATH, SINESTRO.

I DON'T BELIEVE IT.
WHAT?
LOOK.

EEERRRTTT

OH, BOY.
WHAT THE HELL WAS THAT?
IT'S NOT WHAT IT LOOKS LIKE.
JORDAN

IT LOOKS LIKE YOU'RE PLAYING GAMES, MR. JORDAN.
PURPOSELY FLYING BELOW RADAR, REFUSING TO COMMUNICATE.
CAROL--
I MUST'VE BEEN CRAZY TO THINK THIS WAS A GOOD IDEA.

YOU'RE NOT INSANE, CAROL.

IN FACT, YOU HAVE QUITE A BEAUTIFUL MIND.
AMONG OTHER THINGS.
H-HECTOR?
OH MY GOD. WHAT'S HAPPENING?

WHAT'S HAPPENING? I CAN READ YOUR THOUGHTS.

DON'T TOUCH ME!
DON'T YOU SEE, MY DEAR, WHAT A WONDERFUL CONNECTION WE CAN HAVE NOW.

DEEPER THAN ANYTHING ANYONE HAS.
OUR MINDS WILL BE ONE.
AND OUR... OUR...

YOU...

...OH, THIS IS WONDERFUL.
WHAT UNIQUE EXPERIENCES THIS ONE HAS.
HAL JORDAN. I SEE YOUR LIFE.
WHAT A LIFE--

--GREEN LANTERN!

...REVENGE WILL BE MINE.
COAST CITY 66 miles

BOOK FIVE

COAST CITY.
HAND MORTUARY
ROOM 5

HAN
MOR

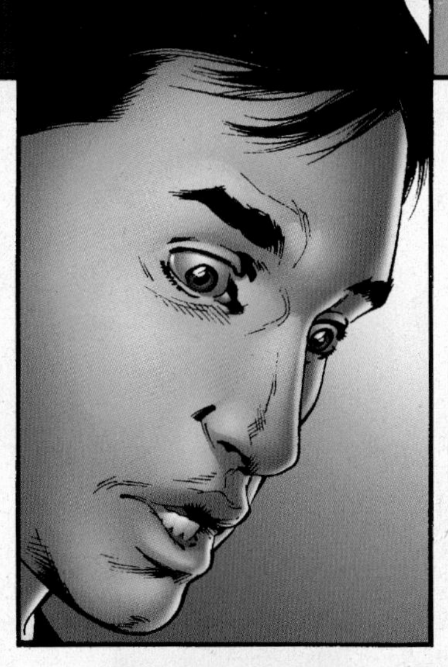

WILLIAM.

YOUR FATHER JUST FINISHED CLEANING THIS ONE UP!
I WASN'T D-D-DOING ANYTHING, MOM! I SWEAR!
HOW MANY TIMES HAVE WE TOLD YOU TO STAY *OUT* OF THE BASEMENT?
I KNOW, BUT...I JUST WANTED TO L-L-LOOK.

WHY? WHY CAN'T YOU BE A *GOOD CHRISTIAN* LIKE YOUR *BROTHERS?*

I DON'T KNOW.

HAL JORDAN.
YOU ARE AN ANGRY MAN.
HIS NAME WAS HECTOR HAMMOND.
HE WAS AN ASTROPHYSICS AND THEORETICAL SCIENCE CONSULTANT FOR FERRIS AIRCRAFT AND THE UNITED STATES AIR FORCE.
I'D LATER FIND OUT HE WAS EXPOSED TO THE METEORITE CORE OF ABIN SUR'S SHIP.
IT AMPLIFIED HIS SICK BRAIN. HIS MIND WAS TELEKINETIC. HE COULD READ OTHERS.
AND HE KNEW ALL OF MY SECRETS.

YOU HAVE MET EXTRA-TERRESTRIALS.
LIFE FAR BEYOND OURS.
THEY GAVE YOU A POWER RING. A BAND OF ENERGY AND WILL.
THEY CALLED IT THE GREATEST WEAPON IN THE UNIVERSE.
THE GREATEST TECHNOLOGY.

HA HA HA HA HA!
GIVE ME THIS EMERALD MIRACLE, HAL JORDAN. GIVE...

...NO.
NO, YOU CAN'T HAVE HER.

NO, CAROL FERRIS IS MINE.
CHRISTINE FERRIS
Loving Wife and Mother

SHE'S MINE!
I DON'T... WANT HER, HAMMOND.

LIAR!
KRRRAKKKK

I SEE YOUR THOUGHTS FLOATING AROUND YOU. EVERY LAYER OF WHO YOU ARE PEELED BACK AND ON DISPLAY.
I SEE THINGS NO ONE ELSE SEES.
YOU'VE LIVED YOUR LIFE TRYING TO PROVE TO EVERYONE THE DEATH OF YOUR FATHER DIDN'T MAKE YOU AFRAID.
IT'S MADE IT SO EXCITING.
BUT YOU HAVEN'T SHARED IT WITH ANYONE.

UNTIL NOW.

I TRIED TO POUR SOME WILL INTO THE RING, BUT IT FELT LIKE IT WAS SLIPPING OFF.
THE BEST I COULD DO--

-- WAS BLIND HIM.
AAAAAAHHH!

CAROL?
YOUR BOYFRIEND'S BACK.
H-HAL?
HAL, WHAT'S GOING ON?

HE'S NOT MY BOYFRIEND.

LOOK AT THAT SHARED TRAUMA.
ALL THE TRAGEDY IN YOUR LIFE, IT'S NO WONDER YOU'RE BOTH SO COLD.

BUT YOU DON'T HAVE TO BE, CAROL. IT'S YOUR CHOICE.

I'M NOT AN UNREASONABLE MAN.

I'M JUST PASSIONATE.
KRAKOOM

YOU ARE ALSO BREAKING THIRTY-FOUR TERRESTRIAL AND INTERGALACTIC LAWS.
CHIEF AMONG THEM, HUMAN, IS ATTACKING AN OFFICER OF THE GREEN LANTERN CORPS.
EVEN IF I DO USE THE TERM *"OFFICER"* LOOSELY.
WHAT?
RING. ***REMOVE*** HIS AIR SUPPLY.

APPROXIMATELY FIVE SECONDS UNTIL THE AIR FROM HIS LUNGS IS EVACUATED.

N-NO. WHO...?
THREE.

ONE.

ASTONISHING.

A RUDIMENTARY TELEPATH LIKE THAT ACTUALLY DISRUPTED YOUR CONCENTRATION?

GREEN... LANTERN?
COME, ROOKIE.

WOOOOSHH

...HAL?

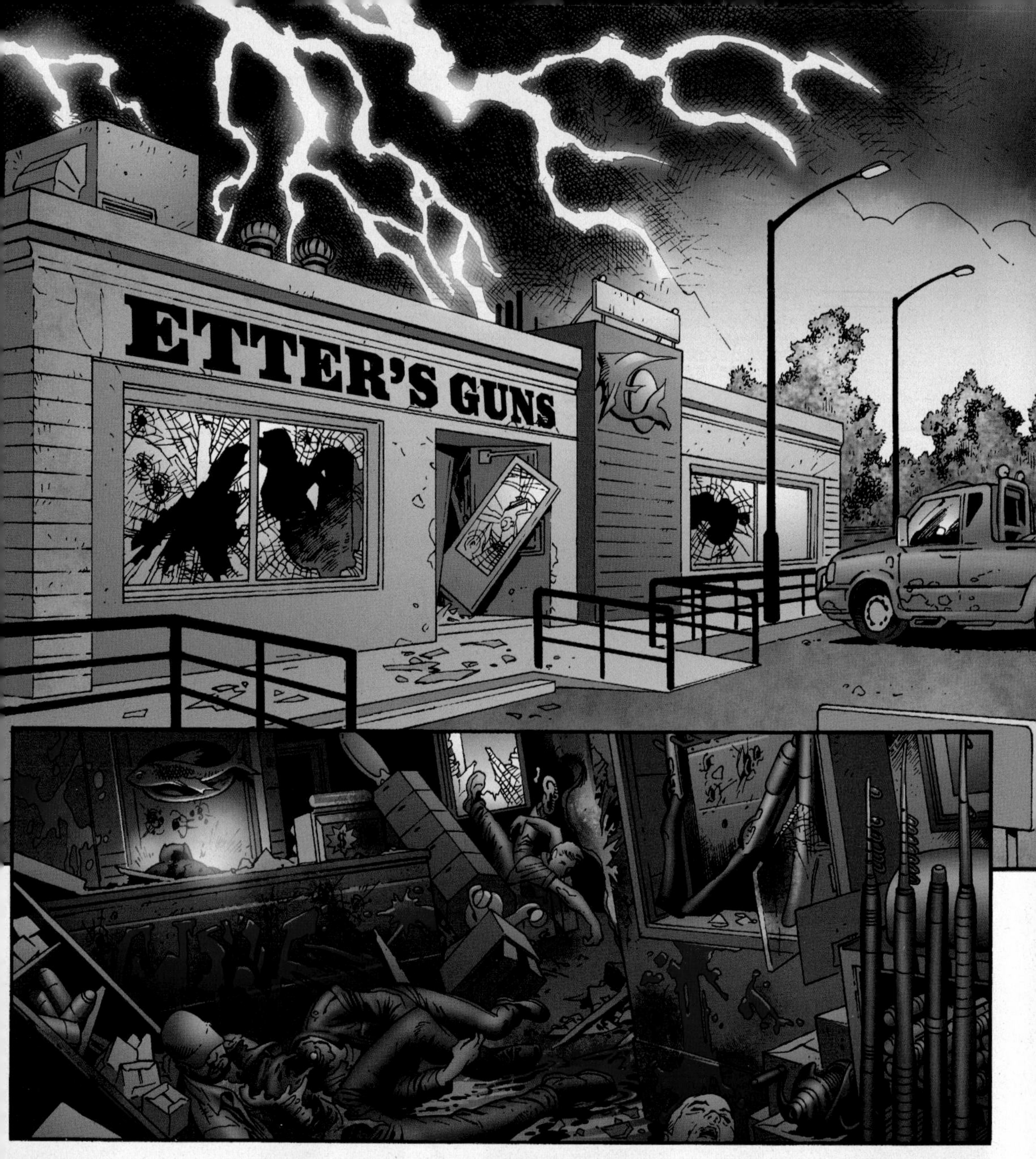
ETTER'S GUNS

YOU WILL CONTAIN THIS POWER OF THE BLACK FOR MY JOURNEY *HOME*.
KRAKT

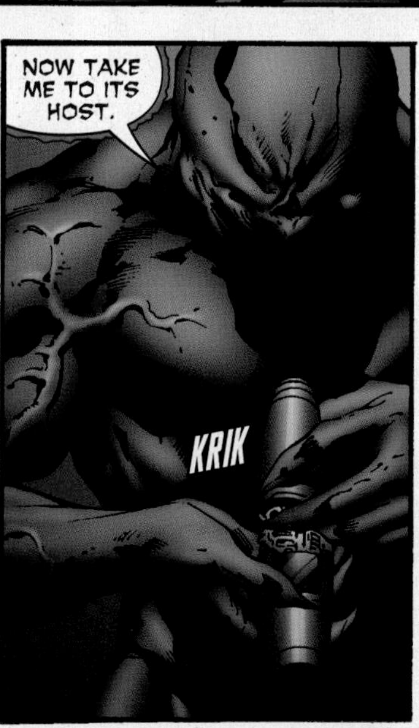
NOW TAKE ME TO ITS HOST.
KRIK

TAKE ME TO *WILLIAM HAND*.
KRIK KRIK KRIK KRIK

...REMOVING THE AIR FROM HIS LUNGS WAS A SIMPLE SOLUTION. WITHOUT IT, HIS TELEKINETIC BRAIN HAD NO CHOICE BUT TO SHUT DOWN.
I WOULD'VE THOUGHT OF THAT.
I DON'T THINK YOU THINK OF ANYTHING, JORDAN. DO YOU EVER PLAN AHEAD?
FOR EXAMPLE: FLYING TODAY.
IF I HAD NOT BROUGHT YOU YOUR RING, YOU WOULD HAVE DIED.
AND YOU WOULD'VE BEEN A MURDERER. YOU WERE THE ONE IN MY FLIGHT PATH.

WHY WOULD YOU EVEN FLY WITHOUT YOUR RING?
I FORGOT IT.
SOMEHOW, I DOUBT THAT.
FINE. LESSON LEARNED. CAN YOU GO NOW? I'VE HAD ALL THE TRAINING I NEED.

KILOWOG TAUGHT ME HOW TO RING SLING.
POORLY.
SALAAK HAD ME TEST THE CHARGING LIMITATIONS.
SALAAK'S "TESTS" ARE WORTHLESS WHEN FACED WITH THE REALITY OF A "DEAD" RING.
AND EVERYONE WARNED ME ABOUT THE YELLOW IMPURITY.

OF COURSE, NO ONE CAN ACTUALLY TELL ME WHAT THAT IS OR WHY IT'S THERE.
IT DOESN'T EVEN MAKE ANY SENSE.
YELLOW.

Hh.
WHAT?
I HAVE BEEN ATTEMPTING TO SEEK THE TRUTH ABOUT THE YELLOW IMPURITY FOR YEARS. I WAS SUSPENDED AFTER ACCUSING THE GUARDIANS OF PUTTING IT THERE THEMSELVES WHEN I WAS A ROOKIE.

DID YOU KNOW HIM?

ABIN SUR WAS MY MENTOR.

I SUPPOSE I QUESTIONED HIM AND DISRESPECTED HIM AS MUCH AS YOU DO ME.
HE SHOWED ME HOW TO TEMPER THAT. AND WHY IT WAS NECESSARY FOR A MEMBER OF THE GREEN LANTERN CORPS.
SO HE TOLD YOU TO SHUT UP AND PLAY GOOD SOLDIER?

OF COURSE NOT. I AM AN INDIVIDUALISTIC THINKER, AS YOU ARE. I'D NEVER BELONGED TO A GROUP LIKE THE CORPS BEFORE.
SO I HAD NEVER LEARNED HOW TO TRUST THE BEINGS AROUND ME.
IN PART, THAT'S WHERE MY QUESTIONING CAME FROM.
HE HELPED ME LEARN TO TRUST MY FELLOW CORPSMAN. THANKFULLY, IT DIDN'T CHANGE MY DRIVE TO SEEK THE TRUTH OR MY DETERMINATION TO ARGUE AGAINST THE THEOLOGIES I DISAGREE WITH.

THEN WHAT DID IT HELP YOU DO, SINESTRO?
SINESTRO. GREEN LANTERN 1417 REGISTERED IN DIRECT VICINITY. MESSAGE 22 UNLOCKED.

MESSAGE READY.
WHAT? WHAT ARE YOU DOING TO MY RING--?
NOTHING. THERE'S SOMETHING IN THERE FOR ME.
RING, PLAYBACK.

GREETINGS, SINESTRO.
MY FRIEND.

ABIN?

I REALIZE I HAVE NOT BEEN AS RIGHTEOUS AND EFFECTIVE AN OFFICER LIKE YOU OF LATE.
BUT THIS TEACHER FEARS NOT BEING SURPASSED BY HIS STUDENT.

YOUR SUCCESS IS ALL I HOPE FOR, SINESTRO.

I HAVE LEARNED THE SECRETS OF LIFE.
AND TO UNDERSTAND THE SEVERITY OF MY MISSION IS TO UNDERSTAND THE GREATEST TRAGEDY THAT HAS EVER BEFALLEN THE UNIVERSE.
A CRIME SO HORRENDOUS AND UNFATHOMABLE, IT IS MYTH.

LONG BEFORE THE GUARDIANS OF THE UNIVERSE RECRUITED SENTIENT LIFE FORMS INTO THE GREEN LANTERN CORPS, THEY CREATED A DIFFERENT POLICE FORCE.
ONE THEY BELIEVED WOULD NEVER BE MANIPULATED BY EMOTION. THE GUARDIANS SAW EMOTION AS A WEAKNESS IN INTELLIGENT LIFE.

THEY CONSTRUCTED THOUSANDS OF ARTIFICIAL SOLDIERS. MANHUNTERS. THEY DISPATCHED THEM ACROSS THE UNIVERSE TO MAINTAIN ORDER.
FOR EONS, THEY DID JUST THAT.

UNTIL THE MASSACRE.

"THE MASSACRE OF SECTOR 666.
"IT HAPPENED IN AN INSTANT. A GLITCH WAS TRIGGERED, ACCIDENTALLY OR WITH PURPOSE, WITHIN THE MANHUNTERS.
"THEY CAME TO THE CONCLUSION THAT THERE COULD ONLY BE ORDER IN OUR UNIVERSE IF LIFE WERE ERADICATED.
"THEY ANNIHILATED WORLD AFTER WORLD. TRILLIONS OF INTELLIGENT BEINGS.

"THERE WERE FIVE SURVIVORS.
"FIVE WITHIN AN ENTIRE SECTOR ONCE FULL OF LIFE."

THOSE FIVE BECAME KNOWN AS THE FIVE INVERSIONS. A TERRORIST CELL BENT ON THE DESTRUCTION OF THE GUARDIANS OF THE UNIVERSE.
CHIEF AMONG THEM, ATROCITUS.
ALONG WITH QULL, THEY SOUGHT THE INNER POWERS OF THE UNIVERSE. WITH THEIR RITUALS AND SACRIFICES, THEY PEERED INTO THE DEEPEST DEPTHS OF THE FUTURE.
AND THEY SAW DARKNESS.
A BLACK SO DEVOID OF LIFE, EVEN THE GUARDIANS' LIGHT COULD NOT PENETRATE IT.
THEY SEEK TO TAKE THIS DARKNESS FOR THEMSELVES AND TURN IT AGAINST US.

IT WAS FORETOLD, THAT POWER WOULD BE FOUND ON EARTH.
I KNOW YOU DO NOT BELIEVE THESE PROPHECIES, SINESTRO, NOR DO THE GUARDIANS. BUT I ASK, IN THE NAME OF OUR FRIENDSHIP, TRUST ME.

YOU MUST STOP THEM FROM UNLEASHING THIS DARKNESS.
IT WILL DESTROY THE UNIVERSE.

HE LOOKED... SCARED--
WHAT?
WHEN YOU SPOKE TO ABIN SUR, DID YOU SEE ANOTHER BODY?
ANOTHER BODY, JORDAN?

ABIN SUR WAS THE ONLY ONE I SAW IN THE SHIP. BUT HE WAS TORE UP PRETTY BAD. I THOUGHT IT WAS FROM THE CRASH. I DIDN'T THINK IT WAS BY SOMEBODY.
IT WAS.
ATROCITUS SURVIVED.

"WE NEED TO FIND HIM."

VISITIN
HOURS
3:30pm
5:30pm

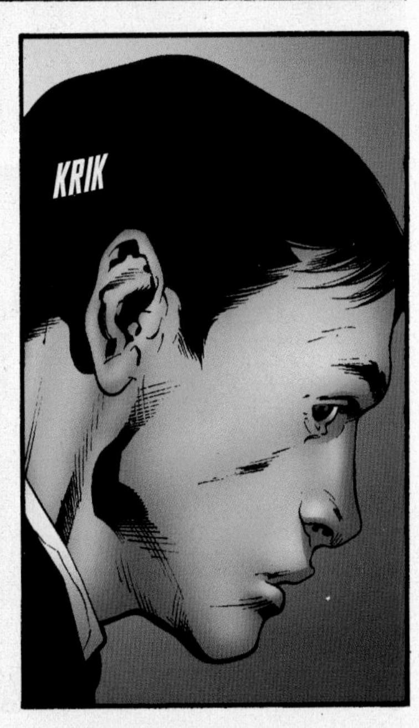
KRIK

KRRRKKKSHH
AAHHH!!

WILLIAM!

RRRROOORRR!

KRIK KRIK KRIK KRIK KRIK KRIK

WILLIAM HAND.
KRIK KRIK KRIK KRIK KRIK KRIK

YOUR INSIDES HOLD THE DOORWAY TO ABSOLUTE *DARKNESS.*
ATROCITUS!

YOU ARE UNDER *ARREST*.
GREEN LANTERNS.
YOU ARE AS *GUILTY* AS YOUR *MASTERS*.

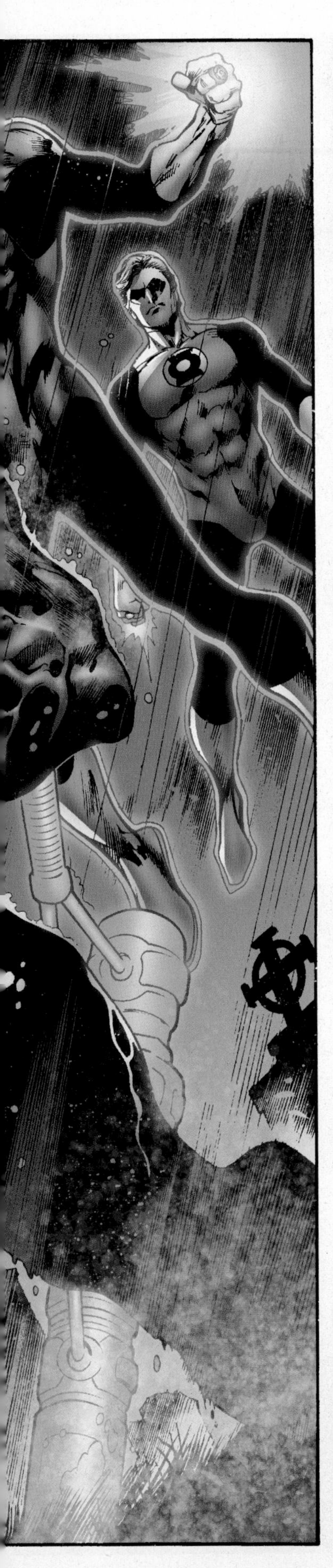

FEEL MY RAGE.

KID! GET OUT OF HERE!

RUN, DAMMIT!

NNGGFF!
WARNING. POWER LEVELS DEPLETING.
POWER LEVELS AT 38.7%

SINESTRO? WHAT'S... HAPPENING?
HE'S BUILT A COSMIC DIVINING ROD.

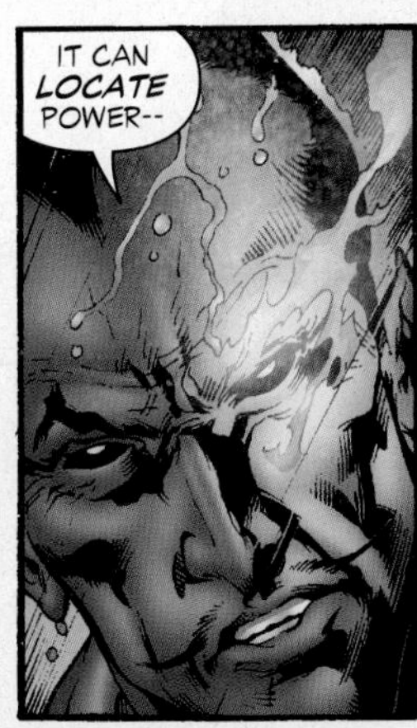
IT CAN LOCATE POWER--

--AND IT CAN TAKE IT.
WARNING. POWER LEVELS APPROACHING 0.0%
GET ON YOUR FEET, JORDAN.

LET'S SEE WHAT YOU'RE MADE OF WITHOUT THAT RING!

SECRET ORIGIN

BOOK SIX

NO ONE ELSE HAD TO WATCH THEIR FATHER DIE IN FRONT OF THEIR EYES.
THAT'S WHAT I THOUGHT MOST OF MY LIFE.
I THOUGHT I WAS ALONE.
GROWING UP, THE PILOTS WHO KNEW DAD WOULD LOOK AT ME WITH PITY WHEN I'D BEG TO GO ON A FLIGHT.
THEY ALWAYS REFUSED.
WHEN I FLEW MYSELF, THEY WOULD LOOK AT ME WITH ANNOYANCE, THINKING I WAS BREAKING THE RULES AND PUSHING THE BOUNDARIES UNTIL THE RIVETS POPPED OFF MY WINGS OUT OF ARROGANCE.
MARTIN JORDAN
JESSICA JORDAN

NO ONE EVER LOOKED AT ME WITH ANY KIND OF UNDERSTANDING.
NO ONE KNEW WHY I WAS THE WAY I WAS.
NOT UNTIL I MET SINESTRO.
JORDAN, FALL BACK.
I'VE NEVER RUN FROM A FIGHT BEFORE, SINESTRO. NOT GONNA START NOW.

YOUR RING IS EMPTY, LANTERN.
YOU ARE NOTHING TO ME.
SSLLAASSHH

GIVE ME YOUR BEST--

GET DOWN
BOOOOM

IDIOT!
SPLAATTT

KRIK
KRIK
KRIK
KRIK
YOU ARE STILL HERE, BOY.
DOORWAY TO THE *BLACK*.

WILLIAM HAND...
...YOUR INSIDES HOLD THE POWER THAT WILL *DESTROY* THE GUARDIANS OF THE UNIVERSE.
YOU ARE THE INCUBATOR OF *DEATH* TO *ALL!*

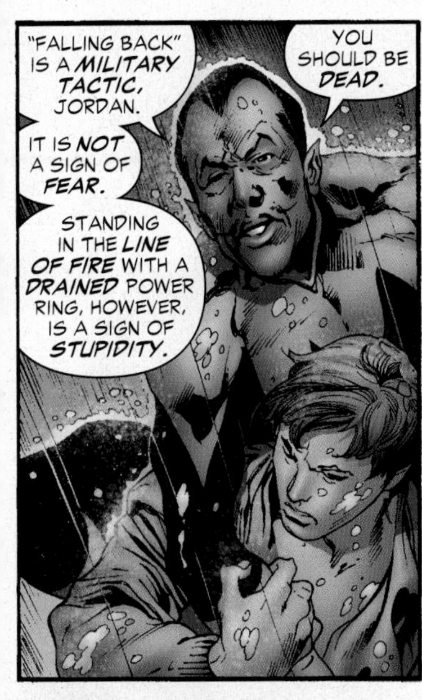
"FALLING BACK" IS A MILITARY TACTIC, JORDAN.
IT IS NOT A SIGN OF FEAR.
STANDING IN THE LINE OF FIRE WITH A DRAINED POWER RING, HOWEVER, IS A SIGN OF STUPIDITY.
YOU SHOULD BE DEAD.

YOU'RE NOT THE FIRST ONE TO TELL ME THAT.

I'M SHOCKED.
THAT DEVICE ATROCITUS IS HOLDING IS CAPABLE OF REMOVING AND CONTAINING THE ENERGY WITHIN OUR RINGS.
WE NEED TO KEEP CLEAR OF IT AND WE NEED TO RECHARGE.

WHAT ARE YOU DOING?
RECALLING MY POWER BATTERY.

DON'T TELL ME SALAAK DIDN'T EDUCATE YOU ON CONFINED POCKET DIMENSIONS AND THE STORAGE OF PERSONAL CHARGING UNITS.

I KEEP MINE IN MY LOCKER.
YOU'VE REDEFINED THE WORD CARELESS FOR ME, JORDAN.

SO I TAUGHT YOU SOMETHING?
JUST LIGHT UP, ROOKIE.

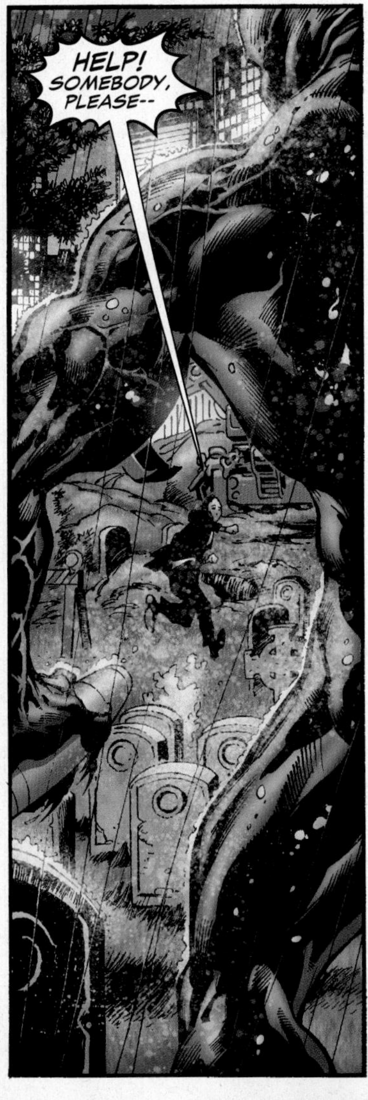
HELP! SOMEBODY, PLEASE--

UnnNFf!

KRRAAATCH!!

I ONLY WANTED TO... I ONLY WANTED TO SEE HOW COLD THEY WERE.
THAT'S ALL!

LEAVE ME ALONE, DEMON!
KRIK KRIK KRIK
YOUR DESTINY AWAITS.

SO DOES YOURS, FELON.

COME ON, JORDAN! STOP WITH THE HANDS AND FORCE SPHERES.
OPEN UP YOUR MIND.
AND STRENGTHEN THOSE CONSTRUCTS.

LET GO OF YOUR ANGER!

A ROOKIE.

BUT YOU...
...I KNOW YOU, LANTERN.
YOU ARE SINESTRO.

OUR PROPHECIES SAY YOU ARE THE GREATEST OF THEM ALL.
THEY SAY IF ANYONE IS TO OPPOSE OUR REVENGE, IT IS YOU.

Nn...

BUT THEY ALSO SAY YOU HAVE A WEAKNESS.
LIKE ALL OF THE GUARDIANS' TERRORISTS.

I WILL BATHE IN YOUR BLOOD, "GREAT ONE."

NO!

YELLOW...?
...THAT WAS...NOT POSSIBLE...

YOU KNOW MY NAME, ATROCITUS?
GOOD.
TELL THE OTHER FOUR OF THE INVERSIONS WHO THEY HAVE TO FEAR.

CHOOOMMM

SINESTRO. THE GREATEST GREEN LANTERN OF THEM ALL.

HEY!

HEY, KID! YOU ALL RIGHT?

HEY--!
LET THE BOY GO, JORDAN.

WHAT DID ATROCITUS WANT WITH HIM?
THEY GAIN POWER THROUGH THE BLOOD OF OTHERS THEY DEEM "DOORWAYS." BEINGS THEY BELIEVE ARE TIED TO THE GREATER FABRIC OF UNIVERSAL POWER.
UTTER NONSENSE.
YOU SAW WHAT I DID, DIDN'T YOU?
WHAT DID YOU DO?

I USED THE RING AGAINST YELLOW.

YOU ASSISTED IN THIS TAKEDOWN AND ARREST, JORDAN, WITHOUT YOUR RING SEEKING A REPLACEMENT.
YOU SURVIVED. THAT'S ENOUGH.
YOU DON'T BELIEVE ME?
YOU DON'T THINK I'VE TRIED TO PIERCE THE SPECTRUM BARRIER? IT IS FUTILE. EVEN FOR ME.
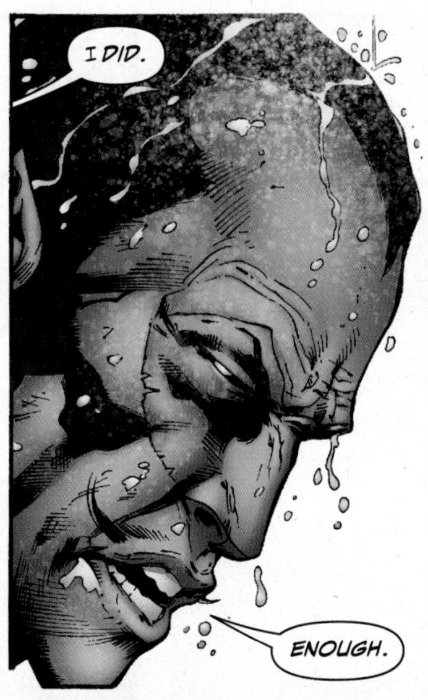
I DID.
ENOUGH.

#$%& YOU.
UNABLE TO TRANSLATE.

HFFF. YOU HAVE TO STAND OUT, DON'T YOU?
YOU CAN'T STAND TO BE UPSTAGED?
BEING A MEMBER OF THE CORPS, YOU'LL NEED TO GET USED TO IT.
WHAT MAKES ANYONE THINK I WANT TO BE AFTER ALL THIS?

YOU NEED TO GET HOLD OF YOUR ANGER, JORDAN. THAT'S WHAT ALMOST GOT YOU KILLED TODAY.
I DON'T KNOW WHAT OR WHO YOU'RE SO ANGRY WITH, BUT YOU CONTINUE TO DIRECT IT AT ME.
YOU NEED TO GROW UP, DEAL WITH IT AND GET ON WITH YOUR LIFE.

YOU KNOW WHAT? I WILL.
RING. TAKE ME TO CARL FERRIS.

JORDAN? JORDAN?!
WE HAVE PROTOCOLS TO FOLLOW!

I DIDN'T LIKE SINESTRO. BUT HE WAS RIGHT. ALL THAT ANGER WASN'T ABOUT HIM.

I THOUGHT IT'D TAKE ME TO A BEACH HOUSE IN FLORIDA...
...INSTEAD I FOUND MYSELF FLYING DOWN TO HIS HOUSE OUTSIDE COAST CITY.

BLUMM BLUMM BLUMM

BLUMM BLUMM BLUMM

JORDAN?

WHAT ARE YOU DOING HERE?
WHERE IS HE, CAROL?
WHO?

YOUR FATHER.

WHERE IS THE OLD MAN?
HE'S NOT--

HE'S HERE.
I KNOW HE IS.

AND I'M GOING TO SEE HIM.
JORDAN, WAIT!

WHERE THE HELL IS HE?
PLEASE, STOP.
FERRIS--?!

WHAT...
...WHAT IS THIS?

HE'S *SICK*.

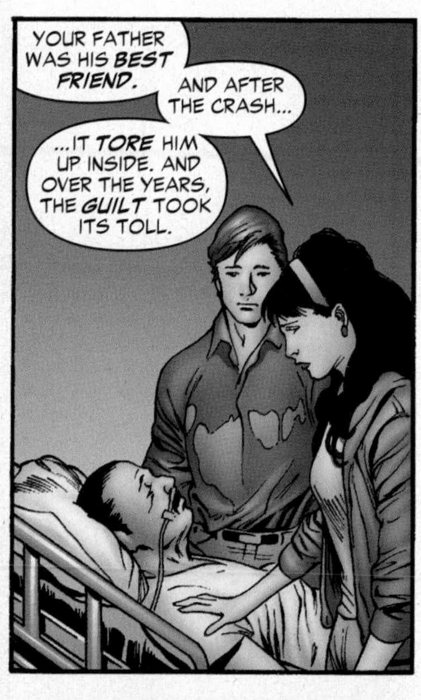
YOUR FATHER WAS HIS BEST FRIEND.
AND AFTER THE CRASH...
...IT TORE HIM UP INSIDE. AND OVER THE YEARS, THE GUILT TOOK ITS TOLL.

HE WAS NEVER GOLFING ON PEBBLE BEACH?
HE'S NEVER PLAYED GOLF IN HIS LIFE.
LAST YEAR, WHEN HE GOT TOO SICK TO GET OUT OF BED, FERRIS AIR WAS ALREADY IN TROUBLE.
SO YOU STOPPED FLYING? YOU STARTED RUNNING FERRIS?
AND YOU LET EVERYONE THINK YOUR FATHER WAS DOING IT ALL THROUGH YOU?

I DIDN'T KNOW WHAT ELSE TO DO.
THAT COMPANY. AFTER MOM AND YOUR FATHER, IT'S ALL HE HAD LEFT.

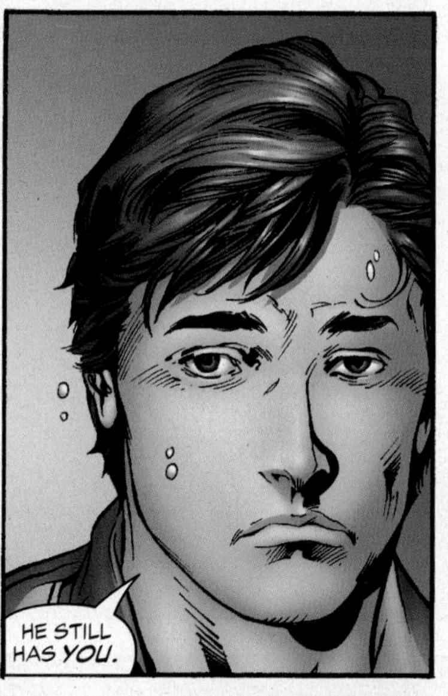
HE STILL HAS YOU.

I WAS A SPOILED BRAT.
WHEN MOM DIED, HE'D GIVE ME ANYTHING I WANTED AS LONG AS I SCREAMED LOUD ENOUGH.
ONE DAY, HE REFUSED. I DON'T EVEN KNOW WHAT I WAS AFTER, BUT I REMEMBER I SAID...
...I SAID I WISHED MOM WAS THERE INSTEAD OF HIM.

HE SAW YOU BRING YOUR DAD A BROWN BAG LUNCH AND HE TOLD ME...
...HE WISHED HE HAD A SON LIKE YOU.

HE WOULDN'T IF HE KNEW ME.
YOU'RE HERE FOR HIM. ME?

I'VE NEVER BEEN THERE FOR ANYONE IN MY FAMILY.

ALL THESE YEARS. ALL THIS TIME. AND I'VE WASTED IT.
I'VE WASTED IT HATING SOMEONE. BEING ANGRY AT SOMEONE.
SOMEONE WHO DIDN'T DESERVE IT.

A LOT OF PEOPLE WHO DIDN'T DESERVE IT.

I'M SORRY, CAROL.

I'M SO SORRY.

JORDAN...
...HAL.

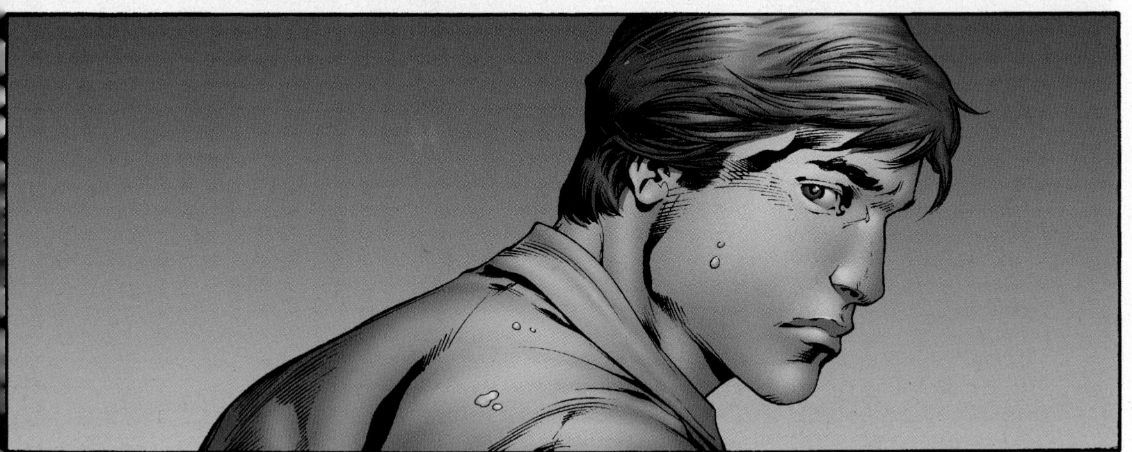

IT'S NOT EASY, IS IT?
WHAT?

BEING ALONE.

YOU'RE NOT ALONE, CAROL.

JORDAN

JORDAN

YOU'VE JUST WITNESSED THE *TRUE* POWER OF THE RING.

IT HAS HELPED YOU FIND THE WILL TO LIVE.
IT IS THE MOST BASIC ELEMENT WITHIN ONE'S WILLPOWER.

YOU WERE RIGHT.

I KNOW.
YOU AREN'T RIGHT ABOUT EVERYTHING.

BUT THE ANGER... THE ANGER I'VE HELD ONTO SINCE I WAS A KID...
...THAT'S BEEN FOR NOTHING. THAT HASN'T HELPED ANYONE.

BERATING YOU IS MY JOB, NOT YOURS.
I MYSELF HAVE SUFFERED LOSS, JORDAN. GREAT LOSS.
WITHOUT ABIN THERE TO HELP ME, I DOUBT THIS RING WOULD STILL BE MINE.

FOR BEINGS LIKE US, OVERCOMING FEAR IS WHAT WE DO BEST. BUT WHEN IT COMES TO GUILT, REGRET... LOSS...
...EVEN GREEN LANTERNS STRUGGLE WITH THOSE.

NEVER FORGET THAT, JORDAN.
ONE DAY YOU MAY NEED TO PASS THAT ON TO A ROOKIE AS I HAVE. AS ABIN DID.
SO YOU THINK I'LL MAKE IT AS LANTERN NOW?
YOU WILL, IF YOU COME TO UNDERSTAND THE HONOR THAT YOU'VE BEEN BESTOWED WITH. IF YOU LEARN THE TRUE MEANING BEHIND THE OATH WE RECITE.
AND IF YOU SPEND SOME TIME OFF THIS BALL OF MUD AND PRIMITIVE CULTURES AND EXPERIENCE THE WONDER OF THE OTHERS IN YOUR SECTOR.
PERHAPS EVEN IN MINE.

THANKS.

YOU ARE WELCOME--
--GREEN LANTERN.
TIME ALLOTMENT EXCEEDED. ILLEGAL FRATERNIZING BETWEEN OFFICERS REGISTERED.
WHAT?
LANTERN 1417.
LANTERN 2814.
YOU HAVE DISOBEYED OUR TERRITORIAL EDICT. YOU WILL REPORT TO OA--
--FOR IMMEDIATE DISCIPLINE.

GREEN LANTERN 35

SECRET ORIGIN
BOOK SEVEN

WHEN I WAS IN THE COCKPIT, I WAS ALWAYS IN CONTROL.
THIS WAS THE SECOND TIME THE POWER RING TOOK CONTROL.
I TOLD MYSELF THERE'D NEVER BE A THIRD.
HAL JORDAN.
GREEN LANTERN OF SPACE SECTOR 2814.
SINESTRO.
GREEN LANTERN OF SPACE SECTOR 1417.
YOU HAVE DISOBEYED OUR TERRITORIAL EDICT.
WHAT NOW?
IT'S THE GUARDIANS.
THEY WANT A WORD WITH US.
THAT DOESN'T SOUND FUN.
RARELY IS ANYTHING "FUN" WHEN IT COMES TO THE GUARDIANS.
SSSSHHHH
WAS SINESTRO WITH THAT--?
THE EARTHMAN.
NFFFF
SINESTRO...

...WHAT DO YOU HAVE TO SAY FOR YOURSELF?
DO US BOTH A FAVOR, JORDAN.
LET ME DO THE TALKING.

YOU ARE WELL AWARE OF THE LIMITS WE HAVE PUT ON THE CONGREGATION OF OUR OFFICERS OFF THE PLANET OA.
THESE ARE THE GUARDIANS OF THE UNIVERSE? THEY'RE SO SMALL--
SHUT UP.
THIS IS THE SECOND TIME YOU HAVE DISOBEYED US. AND AGAIN WITH THE GREEN LANTERN OF SECTOR 2814.
ALBEIT IT A DIFFERENT ONE. THIS IS NOT ABIN SUR.

MY NAME'S HAL JORDAN.

THEY KNOW THAT.
SINESTRO--?

EXPLAIN YOURSELF.

I WAS SIMPLY ASSISTING THIS OFFICER IN LOCATING AND ARRESTING THE KILLER WHO ENDED THE LIFE OF ABIN SUR.
ATROCITUS OF THE FIVE INVERSIONS.
AND BEFORE YOU SO ARROGANTLY RIPPED ME AWAY FROM THAT BACKWARDS BALL OF DIRT, I HAD HIM IN CUSTODY.
WE ARE WELL AWARE.

ATROCITUS WAS TETHERED TO YOUR RING.
THIS TERRORIST WILL BE RETURNED TO YSMAULT WHERE HE WILL CONTINUE HIS SENTENCE--
--AN ETERNITY OF IMPRISONMENT.

HOWEVER, THIS ARREST DOES NOT EXCUSE YOU FROM BREAKING OUR TERRITORIAL EDICT, SINESTRO.
GREEN LANTERNS MUST ONLY OPERATE IN THEIR RESPECTIVE SECTORS. THEY MUST PATROL INDEPENDENTLY. THEY MUST FLY ON THEIR OWN--

WHY?

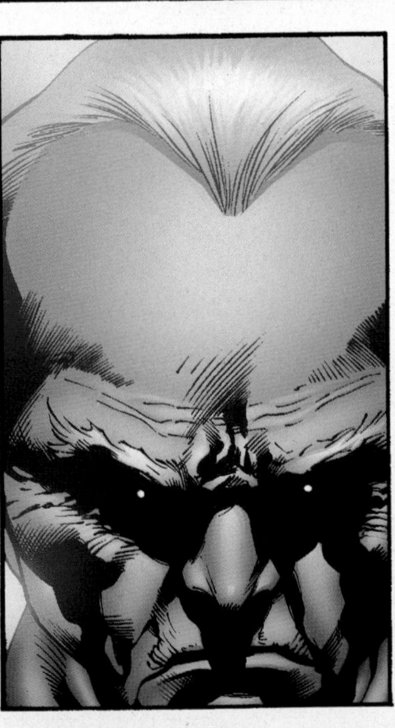

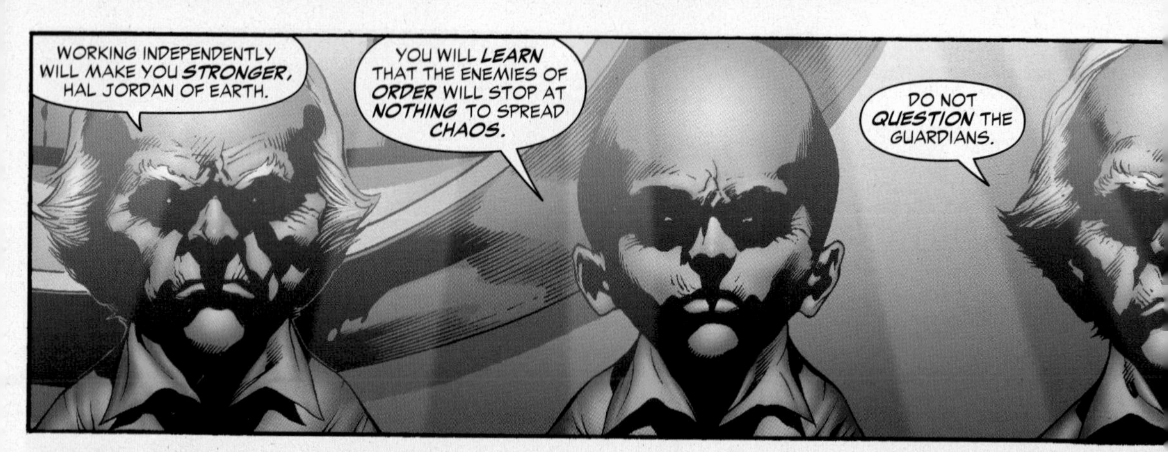
WORKING INDEPENDENTLY WILL MAKE YOU STRONGER, HAL JORDAN OF EARTH.
YOU WILL LEARN THAT THE ENEMIES OF ORDER WILL STOP AT NOTHING TO SPREAD CHAOS.
DO NOT QUESTION THE GUARDIANS.

WHY?

WE HAVE LIVED FOR BILLIONS OF YEARS.

WHAT WE DO, WE DO FOR THE WELL-BEING OF THE ENTIRE UNIVERSE.

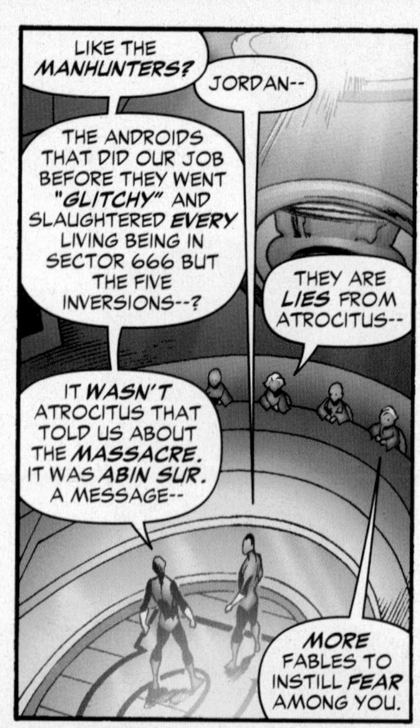
LIKE THE MANHUNTERS?
JORDAN--
THE ANDROIDS THAT DID OUR JOB BEFORE THEY WENT "GLITCHY" AND SLAUGHTERED EVERY LIVING BEING IN SECTOR 666 BUT THE FIVE INVERSIONS--?
THEY ARE LIES FROM ATROCITUS--
IT WASN'T ATROCITUS THAT TOLD US ABOUT THE MASSACRE. IT WAS ABIN SUR. A MESSAGE--
MORE FABLES TO INSTILL FEAR AMONG YOU.

INSTILL FEAR IN US? YOU KNOW WHAT I THINK?
I THINK YOU'RE AFRAID.

YOU DARE ACCUSE THE GUARDIANS OF FEELING FEAR?
JORDAN. DON'T PUSH IT TOO FAR--
I'VE SEEN WORSE LIGHT SHOWS, SINESTRO. I'M NOT AFRAID OF THEM.
BUT I THINK IT'S PRETTY OBVIOUS...
...THAT THEY'RE AFRAID OF US.
THAT'S ABSURD.
OUR RINGS DON'T WORK ON YELLOW, BUT NO ONE CAN EXPLAIN WHY.

"AND THE BUILDINGS ON OA, THE CITADEL OF THE GUARDIANS, THEY ALL JUST HAPPEN TO BE YELLOW?
"BECAUSE THEY'RE AFRAID WE'LL TURN ON THEM LIKE THEIR ROBOTS DID."

THEY EXPECT US TO OVERCOME OUR FEARS.

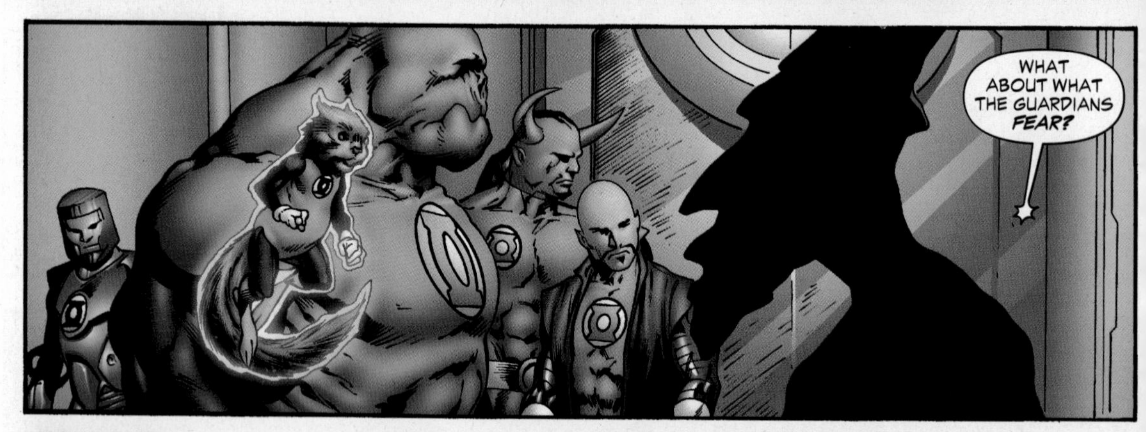
WHAT ABOUT WHAT THE GUARDIANS FEAR?

AND THAT TERRITORIAL EDICT?
THAT EDICT IS $#%?!$%#.
UNABLE TO TRANSLATE.

ENOUGH.
YOUR ACCUSATIONS AND DISRESPECT CAUSE US GREAT CONCERN.
YOU ARE ON THE VERGE OF EXPULSION, HAL JORDAN OF EARTH.

GUARDIANS.
YOU EXPEL JORDAN, YOU CAN HAVE MY RING AS WELL.
OA HELP ME, THE EARTHMAN IS RIGHT.
I AM?
QUIET. PLEASE.

WE CAN BE STRONGER TOGETHER.
THE CORPS SHOULD WORK IN UNISON WHEN NECESSARY.
AND IT SHOULD BE UP TO US TO NOT ONLY HELP OUR FELLOW OFFICERS GROW, BUT TO KEEP THEM IN CHECK. TO INSURE THAT THE TRAGEDY THAT HAPPENED IN SECTOR 666 NEVER HAPPENS AGAIN.

ALL OF THIS. THIS STARTED BECAUSE ONE OF YOU SENT ME TO ASSIST ABIN SUR'S REPLACEMENT.
ONE OF US?
THE ONE WHO CALLS HIMSELF "GANTHET."

"GANTHET"?
WE TAKE NO NAMES.
ONE OF YOU HAS.

WHICH ONE?

I BELIEVE WE HAVE HEARD MUCH TO CONSIDER, SINESTRO. FOR NOW, WE LEAVE THE EARTHMAN WITH HIS RING.
AND OBVIOUSLY, YOU WITH YOURS.

YES. BUT HE IS NOW AS MUCH YOUR RESPONSIBILITY AS KORUGAR AND THE REST OF SECTOR 1417.

WE TRUST THAT IS ACCEPTABLE, SINESTRO...
...GREATEST OF THE GREEN LANTERNS.

Hr.
YES.

"THAT IS ACCEPTABLE."
HNNN!!

FSSSSSSS

I DID DO IT.
YOU DIDN'T DO IT.
I DID.
NO ONE CAN BREAK THROUGH YELLOW, JORDAN. NOT EVEN SINESTRO.
I CAN--
YOU ONLY TRIED LIKE TWENTY TIMES, HUMAN! YOU CAN TRY ANOTHER THOUSAND AND IT WON'T MAKE A DIFFERENCE.
I BELIEVE HIM.

YOU, TOMAR-RE? YOU ALWAYS HAD FAITH FAR TOO READILY.
I SUPPOSE THAT IS ONE THING ABIN TAUGHT ME THAT HE NEVER TAUGHT YOU.

I SUPPOSE...
...I MUST GO.
I DO NOT HAVE TIME FOR ANY MORE GAMES...

...THE GUARDIANS HAVE BOTHERED ME WITH THE *TASK* OF RETURNING ATROCITUS TO YSMAULT.
SINESTRO.

IF YOU'RE GOING TO SAY ANYTHING, JORDAN, SAY "I WON'T MAKE YOU *REGRET* THIS."
I WON'T.
THAT IS ALL I NEED TO HEAR, BECAUSE, *UNFORTUNATELY*, A "GOODBYE" IS NOT APPROPRIATE.

WE WILL RECONVENE IN ONE MONTH SO THAT I MAY EVALUATE YOUR PROGRESS.
BUT *NEXT* TIME--

--YOU'RE COMING TO *MY* WORLD.

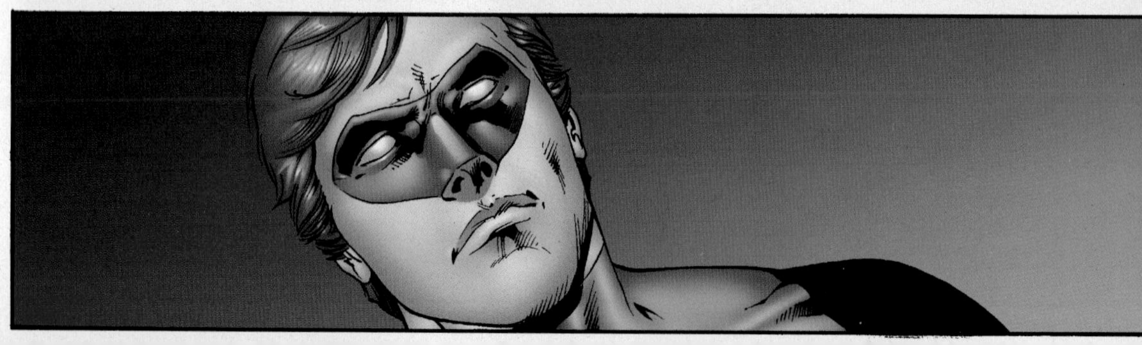

"FERRIS IS LETTING *YOU* FLY?"
"IT'S NOT LIKE SHE HAD MUCH OF A CHOICE, TOM."

I GUESS NOT.
BUT BEING THE ONLY PILOT--
FOR NOW.
BEING THE ONLY PILOT, YOU'RE GOING TO BE LOGGING A HELLUVA LOT OF *FLIGHT TIME.*
24

THAT'S WHAT I'M HOPING.
I STILL DON'T GET WHY YOU WANT TO FLY A *PLANE* WHEN YOU'VE GOT THAT *MAGIC RING.*
THE RING'S NOT *MAGIC.* THE PLANES ARE.
SPEAKING OF. WHICH ONE AM I TAKING UP TODAY?

THAT ONE OVER THERE.

FWUMP

THIS IS...THIS IS THAT HUNK OF JUNK. THIS IS THE PLANE MY DAD FLEW ME IN. BUT--
I'M GOOD, *huh?* ONLY TOOK ME THREE WEEKS.
IT'S AMAZING, TOM.
IT SEEMED LIKE SHE MEANT A LOT TO YOU. I TOLD MISS FERRIS. SHE SAID I COULD FIX IT UP.
CAROL DID?

WHEN EVERY OTHER PILOT *LEFT*, I NEEDED *SOMETHING* TO KEEP YOU HERE.

BUT IT'S MISS FERRIS, JORDAN.
NOT "CAROL."
CIRC

WHAT ARE YOU STARING AT?
HOPEFULLY, THE GIRL I'M HAVING DINNER WITH TONIGHT.
OH, JORDAN. EVERYONE KNOWS--

--I DON'T DATE EMPLOYEES.

GET IN THE AIR.

RIGHT AWAY, MISS FERRIS.

EDWARDS AIR FORCE BASE.
HANGAR 44.
ANYTHING SPECIAL PLANNED TONIGHT?
HEADING DOWN TO PANCHO'S WITH THE GUYS. MY GIRLFRIEND'S BEEN A PAIN LATELY. SHE'S BEEN ON MY CASE ABOUT THE "NEXT LEVEL" OF OUR RELATIONSHIP.
I TOLD HER THE NEXT LEVEL IS ME MOVIN' ON OUT!
I HAVE A GIRLFRIEND TOO.
DO YOU HEAR ME?
44

HELLO?
ANYONE? DO YOU HEAR ME?
YOU CAN'T LEAVE ME IN HERE. THIS IS A TERRIBLY EMPTY PLACE! A VILE PLACE!
I'M NOT LIKE THAT ALIEN SHIP! I'M NOT HERE TO BE POKED AND PRODDED!
DON'T LISTEN TO THE GREEN LANTERN!

HE IS AMAZING THOUGH. THE LIFE HE LIVES IS SO THRILLING.
THE LEAPS AND THE FLIGHTS AND THE WOMEN.
THE WOMEN.
I WANT TO BE A PART OF THAT EXCITEMENT. OH, IT'LL BE WONDERFUL WHEN I AM AGAIN!
YES, OH, YES!

I'M FEELING BETTER ALREADY.

...REPORTS OF MORE STRANGE LIGHTS IN THE SKY ARE POURING IN.
COAST CITY HOSPITAL
CCH

U.F.O.'S? SECRET AIR FORCE TEST FLIGHTS? OR ARE THESE RUMORS OF A GLOWING GREEN MAN TRUE?
IS THE GREEN LANTERN REAL?

WITH THE RECENT APPEARANCE OF SUPERMAN IN METROPOLIS, COULD COAST CITY HAVE ITS VERY OWN PROTECTOR? AN EMERALD WARRIOR--?
KLANK

KLK

CHRIST.
STAND UP. STAND UP AND GET AWAY FROM THAT--
I D-D-DIDN'T DO ANYTHING WRONG.

AWAEE!
FWAASSH

IT'S OKAY. DEAD IS G-G-GOOD.
DEAD IS GOOD.

YSMAULT.
BY ORDER OF THE GUARDIANS, I RETURN YOU TO YOUR CRUCIFIX, ATROCITUS.
YOU ARE TO SERVE OUT THE REMAINDER OF YOUR SENTENCE FOR YOUR CRIMES.
NNYYAAA!

FAREWELL, FELON.
WE WITNESSED THE FATE OF ABIN SUR, SINESTRO!

WE CAN SEE ANOTHER!
YOUR TALES WILL NOT FRIGHTEN ME, QULL. I CAN LOOK OUT FOR MYSELF.
QULL IS NOT SPEAKING OF YOU, SINESTRO. I SEE IT NOW TOO.
AS DO I.

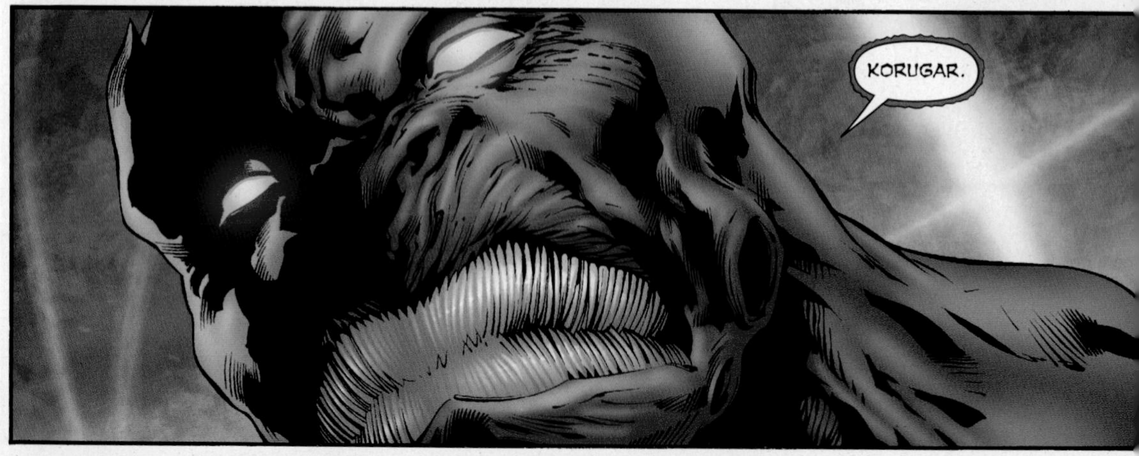
KORUGAR.

YOUR HOMEWORLD WILL SOON DESCEND INTO CIVIL UNREST. VIOLENT RIOTS. A BLOODY COUP.
YOUR PEOPLE WILL PLUNGE INTO MADNESS AS YOU SAVE WORLDS NOT YOUR OWN.

CHAOS WILL SPIN IT OUT OF YOUR CONTROL.

YOU THINK ME A FOOL, ATROCITUS?
KORUGAR WILL NEVER EMBRACE CHAOS. NOT AS LONG AS I AM AROUND TO INSTILL ORDER.

I FEEL NO FEAR, DEMONS.
NO FEAR OF ANY KIND.

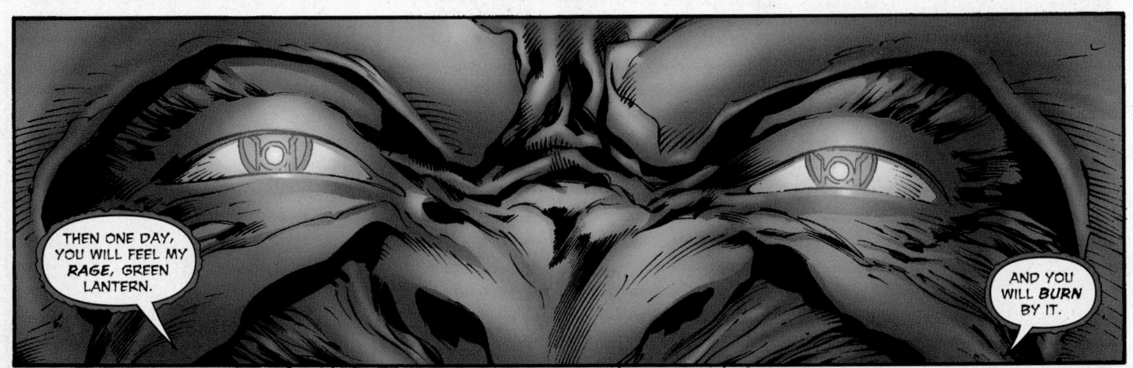
THEN ONE DAY, YOU WILL FEEL MY RAGE, GREEN LANTERN.
AND YOU WILL BURN BY IT.

HAL?

JIM?
JACK'S NOT COMING.
I'M SORRY.
JORDAN

I DIDN'T THINK HE WOULD.
I DON'T **BLAME** HIM. I WOULDN'T HAVE BLAMED YOU **EITHER**.
JORDAN

I'VE **NEVER** BEEN A GOOD **BROTHER**.

THAT'S NOT TRUE, HAL.
IT IS, JIM.
I'VE NEVER OPENED UP AND TALKED TO YOU. NOT EVEN ABOUT DAD.
I NEVER TRIED TO BE A PART OF YOUR LIFE.

BUT I WANT TO BE A PART OF IT, JIM. I WANT TO BE A GOOD BROTHER.

I WANT TO LET YOU IN.

BWOOOOSHHH
HAL?
HAL, WHAT'S GOING ON?

IT'S A LONG STORY.

SO I WROTE IT DOWN FOR YOU.
FLIGHT JOURNAL
THE END